Unequal Prospects

In light of the recent financial crisis and the changing economic landscape, the authors present and analyze the possibility of working longer. Including a range of potential policies (e.g., further increasing the age of eligibility for full Social Security benefits, allocating more government resources to retraining and job search assistance for older workers), this is one of the major approaches currently being discussed by policy analysts inside and outside of the government. Emphasizing the role of inequalities and diversity among older adults, this book provides a framework for thinking about the advantages and disadvantages of working past the current retirement age.

This book is for Sociology of Aging, Social Inequalities, and Social Problems courses.

Tay K. McNamara is a senior research associate at the Sloan Center on Aging & Work at Boston College. Her BA is from Saint Anselm College, and her PhD in sociology is from Boston College. She is the author or co-author of academic articles on a range of topics related to older workers, such as employer-provided flexible work practices, training of older workers, working in retirement, and volunteerism among older adults. These articles have been cross-disciplinary, written for academic audiences in disciplines sharing an interest in aging and work, including gerontology, industrial relations, and human resource management. Additionally, she is a contributor to or author of a number of reports designed to help the media, human resource managers, and other non-academic audiences to understand the results of current research on aging and work. She has also been a speaker or a presenter at webinars and presentations aiming to address the practical implications of these research findings for employer audiences.

John B. Williamson is currently a professor in the Department of Sociology at Boston College. He is also affiliated with the Center for Retirement Research and the Sloan Center on Aging and Work, both at Boston College. His BS degree is from Massachusetts Institute of Technology (MIT) and his PhD is from Harvard University. He has co-authored or co-edited 16 books, many of which deal with aging issues, including two that are gerontology textbooks. He has also authored or co-authored about 140 book chapters and journal articles, many of which deal with aging-related issues such as older workers, retirement, Social Security population aging, and old age security policy in various countries around the world. He was recently Chair of the Social Research, Policy, and Practice Section (which made him also a vice president) of the Gerontological Society of America. He is currently an associate editor of *The Gerontologist* and is on the editorial board of five other journals.

Framing 21st Century Social Issues

The goal of this new, unique Series is to offer readable, teachable "thinking frames" on today's social problems and social issues by leading scholars. These are available for view on http://routledge.custom-gateway.com/routledge-social-issues.html.

For instructors teaching a wide range of courses in the social sciences, the Routledge *Social Issues Collection* now offers the best of both worlds: originally written short texts that provide "overviews" to important social issues *as well as* teachable excerpts from larger works previously published by Routledge and other presses.

As an instructor, click to the website to view the library and decide how to build your custom anthology and which thinking frames to assign. Students can choose to receive the assigned materials in print and/or electronic formats at an affordable price.

Available

Body Problems
Running and Living Long in a Fast-Food Society
Ben Agger

Sex, Drugs, and Death
Addressing Youth Problems in American Society
Tammy Anderson

The Stupidity Epidemic
Worrying About Students, Schools, and America's Future
Joel Best

Empire Versus Democracy
The Triumph of Corporate and Military Power
Carl Boggs

Contentious Identities
Ethnic, Religious, and Nationalist Conflicts in Today's World
Daniel Chirot

The Future of Higher Education
Dan Clawson and Max Page

Waste and Consumption
Capitalism, the Environment, and the Life of Things
Simonetta Falasca-Zamponi

Rapid Climate Change
Causes, Consequences, and Solutions
Scott G. McNall

The Problem of Emotions in Societies
Jonathan H. Turner

Outsourcing the Womb
Race, Class, and Gestational Surrogacy in a Global Market
France Winddance Twine

Changing Times for Black Professionals
Adia Harvey Wingfield

Why Nations Go to War
A Sociology of Military Conflict
Mark P. Worrell

How Ethical Systems Change:
Eugenics, the Final Solution, Bioethics
Sheldon Ekland-Olson and Julie Beicken

Unequal Prospects

Is Working Longer the Answer?

Tay K. McNamara and John B. Williamson

Boston College, Massachusetts

Routledge
Taylor & Francis Group

NEW YORK AND LONDON

First published 2013
by Routledge
711 Third Avenue, New York, NY 10017

Simultaneously published in the UK
by Routledge
2 Park Square, Milton Park, Abingdon, Oxon OX14 4RN

Routledge is an imprint of the Taylor & Francis Group, an informa business

Library of Congress Cataloging-in-Publication Data
McNamara, Tay K.
Unequal prospects : is working longer the answer? / Tay K. McNamara
and John B. Williamson.
   p. cm. — (Framing 21st century social issues)
Includes bibliographical references and index.
1. Retirement age—United States. 2. Population aging—Economic aspects—United
States. I. Williamson, John B. II. Title.
HD7108.4.U6.M36 2013
306.3'80973—dc23   2012031926

ISBN: 978–0–415–52928–0 (pbk)
ISBN: 978–0–203–11793–4 (ebk)

Typeset in Adobe Garamond Pro
by Cenveo Publisher Services

University Readers (www.universityreaders.com): Since 1992, University Readers
has been a leading custom publishing service, providing reasonably priced, copyright-
cleared, course packs, custom textbooks, and custom publishing services in print and
digital formats to thousands of professors nationwide. The Routledge Custom
Gateway provides easy access to thousands of readings from hundreds of books and
articles via an online library. The partnership of University Readers and Routledge
brings custom publishing expertise and deep academic content together to help
professors create perfect course materials that are affordable for students.

Printed and bound in the United States of America
by Edwards Brothers Malloy

Contents

List of Tables

Series Foreword

The world in the early 21st century is beset with problems—a troubled economy, global warming, oil spills, religious and national conflict, poverty, HIV, health problems associated with sedentary lifestyles. Virtually no nation is exempt, and everyone, even in affluent countries, feels the impact of these global issues.

Since its inception in the 19th century, sociology has been the academic discipline dedicated to analyzing social problems. It is still so today. Sociologists offer not only diagnoses; they glimpse solutions, which they then offer to policy makers and citizens who work for a better world. Sociology played a major role in the civil rights movement during the 1960s in helping us to understand racial inequalities and prejudice, and it can play a major role today as we grapple with old and new issues.

This series builds on the giants of sociology, such as Weber, Durkheim, Marx, Parsons, and Mills. It uses their frames, and newer ones, to focus on particular issues of contemporary concern. These books are about the nuts and bolts of social problems, but they are equally about the frames through which we analyze these problems. It is clear by now that there is no single correct way to view the world, but only paradigms, models, which function as lenses through which we peer. For example, in analyzing oil spills and environmental pollution, we can use a frame that views such outcomes as unfortunate results of a reasonable effort to harvest fossil fuels. "Drill, baby, drill" sometimes involves certain costs as pipelines rupture and oil spews forth. Or we could analyze these environmental crises as inevitable outcomes of our effort to dominate nature in the interest of profit. The first frame would solve oil spills with better environmental protection measures and clean-ups, while the second frame would attempt to prevent them altogether, perhaps shifting away from the use of petroleum and natural gas and toward alternative energies that are "green."

These books introduce various frames such as these for viewing social problems. They also highlight debates between social scientists who frame problems differently. The books suggest solutions, both on the macro and micro levels. That is, they suggest what new policies might entail, and they also identify ways in which people, from the ground level, can work toward a better world, changing themselves and their lives and families and providing models of change for others.

Readers do not need an extensive background in academic sociology to benefit from these books. Each book is student-friendly in that we provide glossaries of terms for the uninitiated that are keyed to bolded terms in the text. Each chapter ends with questions for further thought and discussion. The level of each book is accessible to undergraduate students, even as these books offer sophisticated and innovative analyses.

This is the third year of our Routledge social-issues book series. These brief books explore key contemporary social problems in ways that introduce basic concepts in the social sciences, cover key literature in the field, and offer original analyses and diagnoses. Our series includes books on topics ranging widely from global warming, to global ethnic conflict, to comparative health care, to oversharing on the Internet. These readable treatments can be assigned in both lower- and upper-division sociology courses in which instructors seek affordable, pithy treatments for social problems.

Tay McNamara and John Williamson explore a dilemma of our times: Life expectancy has increased because of better health care, diet, and overall wealth, but, as a result, what it means to be "old," and thus of retirement age, has changed. People find their identities in work and don't want to retire. And many simply cannot afford to retire. This intriguing book explores work, retirement, social class, and policy in 21st-century America.

Preface

One of the most pressing and politically controversial social policy issues facing the United States today is how to finance the rapidly increasing burden of paying for Social Security and Medicare. In recent decades there has been a huge increase in our national debt, making it difficult to justify deficit financing to deal with the projected increases in the cost of these programs. Further complicating the situation is evidence that inflation-adjusted wages have been stagnant among lower- and middle-class workers for more than thirty years. Previously, substantial wages were the norm for all income groups; politically, this made it relatively easy to deal with the ever-increasing cost of these and other social programs. The political climate is very different today. Many members of Congress believe that it is far too risky to raise taxes to the extent that would be needed to bring the projected costs of these programs into line with the anticipated increases in the cost of financing these programs. But, then, how are we going to pay for these programs?

Over the past several decades, life expectancy in the United States has increased substantially. At the same time, the proportion of the older population (including those in their mid-sixties through their mid-seventies) who are in relatively good health has continued to increase. This is good news. Were this not the case we would have to conclude that we were doing something very wrong in the United States, because similar trends have been taking place in all of the advanced industrial nations. However, in the United States, as in all other industrial nations, labor force participation rates among older workers continued to decline during most of the post-World War II period. Workers have come to want and to expect to spend final years—hopefully decades—in retirement and free to pursue a variety of leisure activities. Unfortunately, in the coming decades, it will be very difficult to finance long retirements due in large part to projected increases in the costs associated with spending on health and old age pensions.

In this book, we present and carefully analyze the possibility of "working longer." Including a range of potential policies (e.g., further increasing the age of eligibility for full Social Security benefits and allocating more government resources to retraining and job search assistance for older workers), this is one of the major approaches currently being discussed by policy analysts inside and outside of the government. This approach is not entirely new, as legislation associated with the Social Security Reform Act of 1983 set in motion increases in the ages of eligibility for full Social Security pension benefits to be phased in over a period of years. The eligibility age for those full benefits has already increased from age 65 to 66 and within a few years it will increase to age 67. If efforts to encourage people to work longer are successful, it would make a major contribution to our efforts to finance Social Security and Medicare in the decades ahead. However, we believe that it is crucial to take a broad look at the consequences of such efforts. While doing much to solve the projected problem of financing these and other social programs that many older Americans depend upon, we may unintentionally create or exacerbate other problems for them and for society more generally. It is possible that any substantial increase in the retirement age will have adverse consequences; alternatively, it may turn out that how and how rapidly we increase the retirement age will make a big difference.

We have written this book because we anticipate that this issue is destined to receive increasing attention over the next several years. Much will be written about alternative programs and policies designed to keep workers in the labor force longer. Many of the consequences of "working longer" would be beneficial for individuals, such as higher average retirement savings and continued activity that might stave off age-related declines in physical and mental health. However, efforts to keep people "working longer" might also have financial consequences for those who either will not or cannot continue working. Increasing the earliest age at which people can claim early retirement benefits or further increasing the age at which people can claim full retirement benefits would scale back the potential income sources of older adults who are not working and, to some extent, as more focus is placed on encouraging older adults to work longer, programs to encourage later labor force participation (e.g., training and retraining older adults) might receive funding that would otherwise be used on programs to provide a safety net for older adults (e.g., currently, older adults can receive food stamps through the Supplemental Nutrition Assistance program at higher asset levels than younger adults can). Hence, attempts to encourage older adults to work longer might also leave many older adults at risk of inadequate old age security during retirement. We pay particular attention to the likely unequal distribution of some of the effects of such efforts.

In the first chapter we discuss why encouraging older adults to work longer is an important issue today, and will continue to be an important issue in the years ahead. We explore this issue from a variety of perspectives with particular attention to the implications for public policy, for business, and for those with an interest in the potential social impact of changes in this sphere. In the second chapter we focus on the issue of health and wealth inequalities in the United States and their implications for the ability of and need for older workers to remain in the labor force. We give a great deal of attention to how inequality with respect to health and wealth accumulates over the life course. In the third chapter our focus is on the inequality in access to good jobs that older workers face. The choice of occupation and prior **education** as well as health status will be among the factors affecting access to good jobs or, in many cases, to any job at all. In the fourth chapter we take a close look at some potential unintended consequences of efforts to get workers to remain in the labor force longer. What is going to happen if there is a rapid shift toward a much shorter retirement that starts at a much older age than is typical today?

Unlike many other discussions on this topic, this book does not focus on specific policies and programs. It also talks very little about the positive financial effects of encouraging later labor force participation, because most of the positive effects (such as helping to reduce the potential burdens of an aging population and increasing income among older adults who do work) make intuitive sense. Instead, it looks at "working longer" as a general approach, and highlights the ways in which efforts to encourage labor force participation among older adults may have different effects for individuals of different class, race, ethnic, and **gender** groups. It will be difficult to come to a consensus about an equitable distribution of the potential burdens of an aging population. How much of that burden should be placed on older adults through expectations of continued labor force participation? This book does not aim to provide a conclusive answer, but instead to provide a framework for thinking about inequalities that are likely to come into play if we as a society choose to rely heavily on the approach of "working longer." It is distinctly different from many articles and books on this topic in that it addresses how inequalities develop across the life course, beginning in childhood. This approach encourages readers to think about how the inequalities that older workers face develop over time.

Acknowledgments

We would like to thank the reviewers, Harland Prechel, Texas A&M University, and Eric Tranby, University of Delaware, for their helpful comments.

1: An Aging Population: Is Working Longer the Answer?

O ver the course of the 20th century, people retired at younger ages even though they were living longer and often healthier lives. This has produced an unprecedented situation in which large numbers of healthy people are out of the labor force for the last decades of their lives, creating economic and social burdens that we as a society may be ill-equipped to handle. The **economic dependency ratio**—that is, the number of "dependants" (people not in the labor force) for every 100 "workers" (people in the labor force)—provides one way to think about the potential burden that an aging population poses for a society in which early **retirement** is the norm. If the age at which older adults typically retire does not change dramatically, the number of dependent older adults per 100 workers will increase noticeably within the next decade (Toosi 2009). While the number of dependent children will decrease over the same time period, older adults need different goods and services, have different relationships with their families, and need different levels of medical care than children do. Will our economic, political, and social institutions be able to handle the change? If the average American worked longer—delaying retirement for months or years—would the potential problems that an aging population poses be solved? Is "working longer" the answer?

This chapter provides a general overview of work and retirement in an aging population. It outlines some of the reasons why working longer is an important issue and then presents a framework for thinking about whether encouraging people to work to later ages is the answer to the fiscal burdens that population aging poses, in light of inequalities and diversity among older adults.

Work and Retirement in an Aging Population

How did we arrive at a point where "working longer" is a major issue for the future? Over the past century, an aging population, earlier retirements, and better health have led to a situation in which older adults are spending more healthy years out of the labor force.

The United States, like most industrialized nations, has an aging population. In 1980, Americans aged 50 and older made up 26 percent of the population. By 2050, that number will have grown to 37 percent (U.S. Census Bureau 2005). The differences are even more striking when viewed across a longer time frame. In 1900, only 4 percent of Americans were aged 65 or older. By 2008, that percentage had increased to 13 percent (U.S. Census Bureau 2012b). While other factors, such as levels of immigration, play a role, the aging of the population in the United States is in large part the result of three demographic trends: (1) increased life expectancies, (2) decreased **birth rate**s, and (3) the aging of the **baby boom generation**.

First, due to advances in public health and medical science and improved standards of living, people today expect to live longer than their grandparents or even their parents. **Life expectancy**—the average number of years of life remaining at a particular age, such as at birth or at age 65—has steadily increased for more than a century. A white female born at the turn of the 20th century could have expected to live 49 years on average, two years longer than a white male. Minorities could expect many fewer years of life at birth, and many would not survive into their mid-thirties. A black male had a life expectancy at birth of 33 years. A black female would average just one year longer (Shrestha 2006). Today, women still live longer than men, and whites live longer than blacks. However, the similarities end there. Life expectancies at birth in 2010 were 77 years for white males, 82 years for white females, 70 years for black males, and 77 years for black females (U.S. Census Bureau 2012a). To Americans in 1900, the increases in life expectancies that have occurred over just a century would seem implausible. Today, the average life expectancy at age 65 is 19 years (Arias 2011), many years beyond what we would have expected just a century ago.

Second, changes in fertility have fed the long-term trend toward an older population. In 1909, the birth rate—the number of live births per 1,000 people in the population—was 30. By 1999, the birth rate had dropped to half that (Centers for Disease Control and Prevention 1999). The changes occurred in part due to technological advances, such as a shift from horse-drawn farm machinery to tractors and combines, which reduced the incentive for farm families to have large numbers of children. Less human labor was needed. Additionally, as **real wages** increased, children became relatively more expensive because they often prevented at least one parent from being in the labor force full-time (Greenwood and Seshadri 2002).

Third, demographic trends were influenced by the emergence of the baby boom generation. The World War II baby boom, occurring from about 1946 to 1964, was triggered both by high rates of marriage among veterans and by the affluent conditions in the United States following the war—people could afford to have more children. Today, those born during that time period are reaching retirement age and, as they age, the overall **labor force participation rate** is expected to fall due to the larger number of older adults (Toosi 2009). Even without the aging of the baby boom generation, the United States would still be facing an aging population. However, the large number of boomers currently approaching retirement has generated urgency around issues of work and retirement. Because older adults have low rates of labor force participation, the labor force is expected to shrink. In addition to potential labor shortages, this would mean fewer workers paying into programs funded by payroll taxes (such as **Social Security** and **Medicare**) and more people receiving benefits from those programs.

Inventing Retirement: Labor Force Trends

Even as the population ages, the retirement age is lower than it once was. There is evidence that a long-term trend toward earlier retirement is reversing, but the current level of change is projected to be too small to make up for the rate of population aging. In part, the relatively early age at which most people retire reflects the idea of retirement as part of the normal life course. Many people might think of retirement as something that "everyone" does, and question the idea that we can change such a deeply held norm by expecting people to work longer. Historically, however, the idea of retirement as an expected part of the life course is relatively new. A few centuries ago, some people "retired," but the idea of retirement as a stage in the life course when most healthy adults would leave work for a life of relative leisure would have seemed outlandish. Leaving work was reserved for those who were ill, disabled, or unusually well-off financially. Over the course of the 19th and 20th centuries, people began to retire in greater numbers and at earlier ages. Gradually, **social norms** changed to accept retirement as a positive stage in the life course for both men and women (Atchley 1976; Quadagno 1982). As shown in Table 1.1, throughout much of the 20th century, labor force participation continued to decline among older men (Costa 1998). Although the labor force participation rates of women increased over the same period, this was largely due to the influx of women into the labor force in general (Gustman and Steinmeier 2009). Even as life expectancies climbed, people were retiring earlier in their lives.

However, the trend toward earlier retirements began to reverse in the mid-nineties and, by 2010, the labor force participation rate for Americans aged 55 and older had reached 40 percent (Copeland 2011). The century-long decline in the labor force participation rate of older men, followed by the more recent reversal, was due to a range of factors including: (1) the general effects of economic and social conditions; (2) the direct effects of employer and government policies, such as the end of mandatory retirement and the enactment of anti-**discrimination** laws; (3) the effects of the structural incentives embedded in government programs such as Social Security; and (4) the effects of structural incentives embedded in many **employer-sponsored pensions**.

First, economic and social conditions shaped labor force participation. In the wake of World War II, an affluent environment within the United States made retirement

Table 1.1 Labor Force Participation Rate of Adults Aged 55 and Older

Year	Men	Women
1948	70.6	17.2
1949	69.5	18
1950	68.6	18.9
1951	68.2	18.8
1952	67.1	19.3
1953	65.9	19.6
1954	65.7	19.7
1955	64.8	21.6
1956	65.2	22.8
1957	63.4	22.4
1958	62.6	22.6
1959	61.7	23.1
1960	60.9	23.6
1961	60.4	23.9
1962	58.7	23.6
1963	57.7	23.8
1964	57.4	24.3
1965	56.9	24.6
1966	56.5	24.8
1967	56.5	25
1968	56.5	25
1969	56.1	25.5
1970	55.7	25.3
1971	54.7	25.1
1972	53.4	24.5
1973	51.4	23.8
1974	50.7	23
1975	49.4	23.1
1976	47.8	23
1977	47.4	22.9
1978	47.2	23.1
1979	46.6	23.2
1980	45.6	22.8
1981	44.5	22.7
1982	43.8	22.7
1983	43	22.4
1984	41.8	22.2
1985	41	22
1986	40.4	22.1
1987	40.4	22
1988	39.9	22.3
1989	39.6	23
1990	39.4	22.9
1991	38.5	22.6
1992	38.4	22.8
1993	37.7	22.8
1994	37.8	24
1995	37.9	23.9
1996	38.3	23.9
1997	38.9	24.6
1998	39.1	25

1999	39.6	25.6
2000	40.1	26.1
2001	40.9	27
2002	42	28.5
2003	42.6	30
2004	43.2	30.5
2005	44.2	31.4
2006	44.9	32.3
2007	45.2	33.2
2008	46	33.9
2009	46.3	34.7
2010	46.4	35.1
2011	46.3	35.1

Source: Based on the 1948–2010 Current Population Survey

more affordable. People retired in greater numbers and at earlier ages because they could afford to do so. More recent economic recessions have reversed this effect, and many older workers find that they cannot afford to retire with a standard of living that is comfortable to them. One possible response to this predicament is to postpone retirement. Consequently, despite high rates of **unemployment**, the "great recession" that lasted from December 2007 until June 2009 resulted in increased labor force participation among older adults. In the 25 months subsequent to the start of that recession, the number of younger workers (16 to 24) in the labor force decreased by almost one million, but the number of older workers (55 and older) increased by two million (Edwards and Shierholz 2010). Not all of these older workers are employed. In fact, the proportion of older adults who were unemployed grew from 2007 to 2011 (GAO 2011). However, when both the employed and those actively seeking work were counted, it was evident that the recession had caused people to delay retirement.

Second, some employer and government policies, such as **mandatory retirement** and anti-discrimination laws, directly shaped labor force participation rates. Until the seventies, **age discrimination** was a normal and expected part of the workplace in the form of mandatory retirement policies. People were often required to retire at a specific age, such as at age 65. The adoption of the **Age Discrimination in Employment Act (ADEA)** of 1967 made overt age discrimination, at first among workers ages 40 to 65 (Neumark 2009) and later among all workers ages 40 and older, illegal. One of the primary effects of the ADEA was to outlaw mandatory retirement for most industries, leading to increased labor force participation among older adults (Neumark and Stock 1999).

Third, the structure of government programs, such as **Social Security**, influenced retirement decisions. In general, Social Security enabled many older adults to retire. However, beginning in 1940, it also discouraged continued work through the earnings test. An older worker's benefits were reduced in proportion to how much money they earned on their jobs, in excess of a low "exempt" amount of earnings. Beginning in the

1970s, gradual changes made the earnings test less harsh for those who continued working, but as recently as the 1990s a worker over the age of 65 "lost" $1 out of every $2 earned above $9,120 (Friedberg 2000). Technically, if a worker's Social Security benefits were reduced due to the earnings test, they would be compensated through higher benefits later in life. However, people usually perceived the earnings test as a pure tax on their earnings and were reluctant to continue working (Mastrobuoni 2006). In 2000, the earnings test was eliminated for Social Security beneficiaries over the normal retirement age (i.e., 65 to 67 depending on their birth year), leading to increased labor force participation among groups such as men with a high-school degree and high earners (Engelhardt and Kumar 2007).

Fourth, the indirect effects of the structure of employer practices, such as employer-sponsored pensions, went hand-in-hand with changes in Social Security policy. The post-World War II economic climate allowed for the rapid spread of employer pension plans as expected elements of a good job (Gonyea 2007). Most of these were **defined-benefit pension** plans that provided workers with a specific amount of money per month during retirement. In general, the amount of the promised payments increased steadily over the first 25 to 30 years of employment, then more slowly or not at all if the employee chose to work longer (Friedberg and Webb 2005). In some cases, if a person continued working beyond a certain number of years, they would lose money because their extra wages for that year would not outweigh the negative effects on their pension (Burkhauser and Quinn 1997). Hence, from the 1950s to the 1980s, defined-benefit pensions acted as a powerful incentive to retire at the "right" time. However, from the 1980s forward, increasing numbers of employers offered defined-contribution pension plans, in which employers and employees contributed to an account balance, rather than to defined-benefit pension plans. Defined-benefit pension plans were ill-suited to a reality in which fewer workers expected to remain at the same company for 25 to 30 years, and by the early 2000s, three out of four workers with pensions had **defined-contribution pension** plans (Even and MacPherson 2007). In addition to being portable, these plans did not penalize workers for remaining with an organization beyond a certain age.

Many people take for granted that they will retire in their mid-sixties or even earlier. However, the "typical" or expected retirement age has been in flux over the course of the past century. In recent years the trend has been for people to remain in the labor force longer, but the projected increases in labor force participation among older adults are likely to be too small to compensate fully for our aging population.

Why is Working Longer an Important Issue?

The reasons for encouraging people to work longer are usually thought of as primarily economic, aiming to reduce the potential economic burdens of a large nonworking population. By this logic, having people work longer might reduce the imbalances that an aging population would cause in the budgets of government programs such as Medicare and Social Security, as well as reducing **poverty** among the elderly. From a public policy perspective, the question of whether people should work longer is important in at least two ways: (1) the largely positive effects on the revenues of programs funded through payroll taxes, such as Social Security; and (2) the mixed effects on policies such as the Age Discrimination in Employment Act (ADEA). First, numerous government programs are funded directly or indirectly through payroll taxes. The longer that older adults work, the longer they will contribute to the revenues of those programs. In some cases, these additional taxes could help eliminate projected shortfalls in the budgets of the programs. For example, according to current projections the Social Security trust fund (i.e., the amount the program has "saved" from previous years) will be exhausted by 2036 (Board of Trustees 2011). However, many older adults are largely reliant on Social Security for their **income**. For instance, it accounts for 70 percent or more of the cash income of most poor and near-poor adults ages 65 and older (Issa and Zedlewski 2011), and among all adults ages 65 and older it provides four times the income that employer pensions do (Social Security Administration 2011). Potentially, delaying retirement could lead to scenarios in which more older adults could afford to live with lower Social Security benefits (through additional wage income), in which older adults contributed to government programs longer (through additional payroll taxes), or both. Second, the design of other government policies, such as the ADEA, may be less effective for an aging workforce. If certain organizations become dominated by older workers, legislation may need to be adjusted to account for discrimination against younger workers. Currently, members of dominant or majority groups (such as men) can claim reverse discrimination under Title VII of the Civil Rights Act (i.e., **race**, color, religion, sex, or national origin). In contrast, the Employment Opportunity Commission (EEOC) considers favoring older workers over younger workers acceptable under existing federal legislation.

The effects of working longer would extend beyond public policy. For instance, from a business perspective, working longer is an important issue on four levels: the effects on overall human resource strategies; the extent to which an aging workforce may render existing human resource strategies largely ineffective; the potential that age diversity may shape employee interactions; and the unintentional effects on younger workers if older workers remain in the labor force longer. First, in terms of overall human resource strategies, employers may need to balance **knowledge drain** (caused by early retirement) against increased benefit and payroll costs (caused by later retirement). First, working longer may indirectly help employers to prevent knowledge drain, the loss of accumulated knowledge held disproportionately by more established workers within an organization. In a 2009 survey, 74 percent of employers said that they were concerned about the potential for knowledge drain as older workers retired (MetLife 2009b). Employer efforts to prevent knowledge drain would need to be balanced against the potential costs of older workers. Second, specific wide spread human resource strategies might not be suited to an aging workforce. Typically, older employees have received less training than younger employers (Eyster, Johnson, and Toder 2008). Partly, this is because employers expect older employees to leave the organization sooner than younger employees, resulting in lower returns on investment for any training provided (Rix 1996). However, another reason that older employees receive less training is that it is more difficult to design effective training programs for older workers. Younger workers, who are often new to their careers, can be trained through generic programs designed to impart basic skills. Older workers, in contrast, have generally mastered basic skills and would only benefit from customized training methods aimed to specifically sharpen the specific skills that they need (Callahan, Kiker, and Cross 2003). Third, if people remain at work longer, the workplace is likely to become even more age diverse than it is today, raising questions about potential intergenerational conflict. Finally, delayed retirement for older workers may impact the opportunities available to younger workers in both positive and negative ways. On one hand, younger workers often look to older workers for professional advice, mentoring, and advice on how to operate within the workplace (Hewlett, et al. 2009). However, by not retiring, older workers are also occupying jobs, potentially preventing younger workers from gaining employment or promotions.

Unequal Prospects for Older Americans

What do you think of when you picture a "typical" older adult? Are they male or female? Are they a member of an ethnic minority? Are they in good health, or are they frail? Do they struggle financially, or have they saved enough for retirement? Today, older adults are so diverse that no matter what "typical" person you have pictured, they are not fully representative of older adults. This book looks at how the consequences of working longer would differ depending on both in ascribed characteristics (such as race, **ethnicity**, and gender) and in characteristics that are generally acquired over time (such as **health** and wealth).

The U.S. population is becoming more diverse in terms of race and ethnicity. Since the turn of the 21st century, increasing numbers of older adults have been members of racial and ethnic minorities. As of 2010, one in five adults aged 65 or older was part of an ethnic or racial minority. By 2050, that proportion will have more than doubled (Vincent and Velkoff 2010). These changes are being fueled by changes in the life expectancies of older adults from different ethnic and racial backgrounds. In 2007, the gaps between the life expectancies of blacks and whites were the smallest on record (Xu, et al. 2010). Two of the fastest-growing groups of older adults are people of Hispanic descent and people of Asian descent. From 2007 to 2050, the number of Hispanics aged 50 to 69 is expected to quadruple, from less than six million to more than 22 million (Johnson and Soto 2009). The older population is also disproportionately female. Men tend to have higher mortality throughout the life course, and with increasing age the number of women relative to men in the population grows. For example, there are about 136 women aged 65 and older per 100 men in the same age group (Administration on Aging 2010).

As the gender, ethnic, and racial composition of the older population changes, the differences among these groups are likely to become more important. In particular, their health status and **financial resources** tend to differ. Inequalities in acquired characteristics—such as health and wealth—develop over a person's lifetime. By the time people reach retirement age, even if they start life from similar foundations, their outcomes can be very different. Although there is some evidence that older adults are on average in better health than in the past (Helman, et al. 2008), health remains a large barrier to continued work. Similarly, wealth inequalities start early in life and continue through the retirement years. Because financial resources affect access to other types of resources, including education and health care, inequalities in wealth tend to be relatively stable or to increase (rather than decrease) over time.

Conclusion

This chapter has laid the groundwork for understanding why the idea of older Americans working longer is both an important issue and a complicated one. The population of the United States, like that of other industrialized nations, is aging. However, due partly to the influence of public policies such as Social Security and employer provisions such as defined-benefit pension programs, most people expect to retire in their early to mid-sixties. If people continue to retire in their sixties in light of longer life expectancies, it will not be uncommon for people to spend decades in retirement. Working longer could help to counteract the potential imbalances in the budgets of programs such as Social Security, but its consequences extend beyond public policy.

DISCUSSION QUESTIONS

1. What were some of the changes that have been made in Social Security policy over the years that seem to have had an effect on trends in labor force participation rates among older workers in the United States?

2. What are some of the advantages and disadvantages of defined-benefit pensions? What are some of the advantages and disadvantages of defined-contribution pensions for the worker?

3. What are some of the sources of "unequal prospects" for older Americans? Do economic and health inequalities among older adults, as opposed to younger adults, have different effects?

II: Health and Wealth: Cumulative Inequality across the Life Course

One of the major reasons to encourage people to remain in the labor force at later ages is the idea that working longer might provide much-needed income to older workers who could not otherwise afford to retire. People often miscalculate the amount of money that they will need in order to maintain their standard of living in retirement or are simply unable, for various reasons, to save something like the required amount; if they work several years longer, problems associated with low retirement income might be alleviated. However, an underlying assumption behind this is that the people who need additional financial resources will also *be able* to work. To the extent that inequalities in health and wealth go hand-in-hand, many of the people most in need of additional income may not be healthy enough to work.

There is reason to believe that health and wealth inequalities are strongly related. In general, disadvantaged children grow up into disadvantaged adults. "**Cumulative inequality**" refers to the idea that inequalities—both in advantages and in disadvantages—tend to accumulate from childhood to old age. Both upward and downward mobility are possible. The idea that people can go from "rags to riches," overcoming the disadvantages of their earlier lives, is central to the American Dream. However, most existing research suggests that while some people can and do end up significantly better (or worse) off than their parents, the link between the status of parents and children is stronger in the United States than in most other industrialized nations (Corak 2006). In terms of wealth, children from poor households go to less well-funded schools; graduates of less well-funded schools get lower-paying jobs; and workers in lower-paying jobs save less for retirement. Similarly, for health, infants born to mothers with poor nutrition are more likely to have health problems in childhood, and children with health problems are more likely to have **functional limitations** as adults. Why are inequalities in health and wealth so persistent over time? Cumulative inequality occurs due both to increased opportunities among people with advantages and to increased risks among people with disadvantages (Ferraro and Shippee 2009). Individuals who have advantages (e.g., access to better pension plans and medical care) will have more opportunities to reach retirement age able either to retire comfortably due to increased savings or able to work longer due to greater employment opportunities and better health. Individuals who have disadvantages (e.g., low wages, lack of health insurance) will be at greater risk of experiencing job loss, chronic illness, or other events that will cause them to reach retirement age with inadequate health, inadequate financial resources, or both.

This chapter uses the framework of cumulative inequality to explain how inequalities in health and wealth develop over a lifetime, and to provide insight into why they are so strongly related. It first discusses inequalities in health, with emphasis on the factors that lead racial and ethnic minorities and low-wage workers to have less ability to work during the retirement years. It then addresses the corresponding differences in wealth, tracing why some people are more able to afford to retire than others. The focus of this chapter is not on the retirement years, but on understanding the diversity in economic resources and health status that exist when workers enter their retirement years.

Health: Unequal Chances to Work

Poor health can limit people's ability to work, no matter their age. For example, in 2009, 19 percent of people with a **disability**—such as difficulty with vision, hearing, or movement—were employed, compared to 65 percent of those without a disability (Bureau of Labor Statistics 2010c). The effect of health on labor force participation among retirement-aged adults is particularly strong both because social norms expect older adults to be out of the labor force and because older adults are more likely to obtain income through programs such as Social Security. Workers who are in poor health often retire earlier than they would have planned (Helman, et al. 2008). Further, when they retire from their career job—the job at which they have worked for a substantial number of years—workers who are in good or excellent health are likely to work for pay at another job. Those who are in fair or poor health are comparatively more likely to retire altogether (Cahill, Giandrea, and Quinn 2007).

Given the connection between health and work, if older adults were healthier longer, they might be able to work longer as well. And, at least as compared to earlier generations, older adults are relatively healthy. They are typically in better health than their parents or grandparents. As life expectancies have increased, **healthy life expectancies**—the number of years that people can expect to live in full health—have increased as well. For instance, at age 60, when many people plan to retire within the next few years, men are expected to live in full health for 15 years and women are expected to live in full health for 18 years (World Health Organization 2004). Even within the past 20 years, the percentage of older people with functional limitations and disabilities has declined substantially. About three out of four people aged 54 and older rate their health as good, very good, or excellent. Rates of functional limitations (i.e., the health problems that interfere with people's daily lives) have decreased modestly over the past 15 to 20 years (from 49 percent of people aged 65 and older in 1992 to 42 percent in 2007) (Federal Interagency Forum on Aging-Related Statistics 2010).

Despite the increasing average health of older Americans, health is not distributed evenly and there are still many older adults in poor health. Rates of disability increase steadily with age, with over half of people aged 65 and older reporting a disability (Centers for Disease Control and Prevention 2009; Holmes, et al. 2009; Johnson, Favreault, and Mommaerts 2009). Over a long enough life span, many people reach the point at which they are not in adequate health to do strenuous work, or any work at all. However, while some people do not reach that point for years after the typical retirement age, others find themselves in poor health at or even before the age at which they would begin receiving pensions or Social Security benefits. Poor health and disability is concentrated among women, minorities, and those low in **socioeconomic status**. For instance, white women are generally in better health than black or Hispanic women. They are also less likely to experience decreases in health in midlife that would make retirement necessary (Lee and Shaw 2008). These differences in health evolve both as a result of (1) childhood experiences and (2) differential risks and care in adulthood.

Unhealthy for Life? The Influence of Childhood Experiences

Health is strongly influenced by conditions that occur early in life. Even before birth, maternal nutrition and possible substance abuse affect the development of tissues that influence rates of **morbidity**—disability or poor health—in adulthood (Haas and Rohlfsen 2010). Children living in poor families encounter a disproportionate number of risk factors at critical developmental periods. A lack of financial resources directly interferes with the ability of families to provide adequate shelter, health care, and nutrition to children. Other risk factors are more subtle. Poverty is associated with strain on marriages and families and depression (O'Berg 2003), and children who experience physical or psychological violence are likely to have poorer mental health in adulthood (Greenfield and Marks 2010). Both psychologically and physically, children living in poor families are less likely to grow up to be healthy adults.

A number of studies have followed people from childhood to adulthood, and found that deprivation during childhood is associated with low levels of physical functioning in adulthood. For instance, one study based on data from the United Kingdom found that children with less educated fathers reported lower physical functioning during middle age, while the children of more educated mothers reported higher physical functioning during middle age (Guralnik, et al. 2006). A different study based on retirement age adults within the United States found that older adults who had been in poor health or experienced socioeconomic disadvantages as children had more functional limitations (e.g., limitation in the ability to climb a flight of stairs) when they reached their fifties and sixties, as compared to adults from more advantaged backgrounds. For most people in the study, the number of functional limitations that they reported increased with age, but the rate of increase was higher for those who had disadvantaged childhoods (Haas 2008). Hence, people from disadvantaged childhoods not only arrive at retirement age in worse health, their health deteriorates more rapidly during the retirement years.

How much can the health trajectories that result from childhood deprivation be changed in adulthood? There is no clear agreement about how malleable health is after the critical periods in early development. On the one hand, exposure to chemicals or environmental hazards as a young child can manifest in disease during mid- or late life, even with the best health care and behavior. However, there is also evidence that many of the effects of childhood health risks are cumulative with risks in adulthood. If only part of the effect of childhood adversity on adult health is a direct, biological effect, proper medical care and health behavior in adulthood should mitigate negative effects of childhood deprivation.

Health Differences in Adulthood

Childhood deprivation is a powerful influence on people's ability to work during the retirement years. Most evidence would suggest that medical care can mitigate the negative effects of deprivation, both through direct treatment of conditions (e.g., medication for high cholesterol) and through preventative care (e.g., advice on diet). In general, however, people who have experienced childhood deprivation do not have access to the amount and type of medical care needed throughout adulthood. Children with health problems are likely to experience more health risks in adulthood (Haas 2008) but are less likely to have the health insurance they would need to receive adequate treatment. Disproportionate numbers of older adults in poor health are members of racial minorities or women. Blacks have poorer health than whites in part due to the disparities between the average economic resources of the two groups. However, even when differences in socioeconomic resources are taken into account, the race gap remains, in part because racial minorities are not always as successful in translating socioeconomic resources into good health (Shuey and Willson 2008).

Not all employers offer health insurance, particularly to low-wage workers, women, and minorities. Among the lowest-wage workers, only 26 percent have access to medical benefits through their workplaces, compared to 92 percent of the highest wage categories (Bureau of Labor Statistics 2010a). Similarly, in large part due to the concentration of ethnic and racial minorities in low-wage jobs, minorities are less likely to have access to health insurance through their employers. Only about 49 percent of older Hispanic workers have health benefits through their employer, substantially less than the percentages of non-Hispanics whites (65 percent) and non-Hispanic blacks (62 percent) (Johnson and Soto 2009). Additionally, only 80 percent of women (compared to 91 percent of men) have health insurance through their employers. While these women tend to be covered through their husbands' insurances (Bond, J. T. et al. 2005), the concentration of women in jobs that do not provide health insurance poses a problem for divorced, widowed, or never-married women.

Even when workers have access to health insurance plans through their employers, they do not always participate, particularly if it lowers their take-home pay. Nonparticipation in health insurance plans is highest among minorities, low-wage workers, and younger adults. While a large part of the lack of health insurance among Hispanics is attributable to their employers not offering a plan at all (Johnson and Soto 2009), blacks and whites who do not have employer-provided health insurance are more likely to say that they opted not to participate (Fronstin 2007).

Wealth: Unequal Chances to Retire

Wealth strongly affects people's ability to retire. While most older workers enjoy their work, perhaps the single most common reason that people continue to work during their fifties, sixties, and beyond is financial necessity (Helman, Copeland, and VanDerhei 2009; MetLife 2009a). As recently as the early nineties, a relatively high number of people could afford to retire comfortably, at a level of financial resources comparable to what they had experienced during their working lives. Only approximately one in five households approaching retirement age lacked the resources to maintain their standard of living in retirement. Consequent of factors such as changing pension plans and interest rates, the estimated proportion of households who could not afford to retire comfortably had increased to about one in three by 2004 (Munnell, Webb, and Golub-Sass 2007). One analysis of the Survey of Consumer Finances, for instance, found that the average amounts of debt of near-retirees had more than doubled from 1995 to 2004 (Anguelov and Tamborini 2009). The financial crisis of 2007 and the subsequent recession exacerbated this gap, as many workers faced substantial decreases in their retirement savings at the point when they would have begun to tap into these resources. Today, many older workers cannot afford to retire without noticeable decreases in their standards of living.

The chances that a person will need to work in retirement to maintain an acceptable standard of living are unequally distributed because of wide variations in retirement savings. Although the median income of Americans aged 65 and older was $18,208 in 2008, one in four received less than $11,139 per year and another one in four received $33,677 or more a year (Purcell 2009). The people near the bottom of the distribution are disproportionately women or minorities. Women who are single or divorced are more likely to need to work during their retirement years, as compared to men (DeLong 2006), and the recent economic downturn has had large effects on their retirement prospects due to the adverse effects on their savings (Thayer 2008). Black and Hispanic women are at particular risk. One 2008 analysis of data from the National Longitudinal Survey of Mature Women found that the poverty rate of black women was three times that of white women during their retirement years (Lee and Shaw 2008). People with low or no retirement savings are especially vulnerable to risk and uncertainty. Unexpected medical expenses, for instance, can quickly erode their savings far below the amounts needed to retire. These differences in wealth evolve over the life course, due to factors such as (1) differential educational opportunities, (2) differences in pension wealth, and (3) interrupted labor force participation.

Inequalities throughout the Life Course: Poverty and Education

Children who are born into poverty tend to remain in poverty throughout their child-hoods, and **persistent poverty** (as opposed to **intermittent poverty** in which families fall below the poverty line occasionally) strongly affects financial resources as an adult. Generally, the longer a child is poor during childhood, the more persistent the negative consequences are in adulthood. Some disadvantages are evident during their teenage years, when they are less likely to graduate high school and are more likely to become unmarried parents. Other disadvantages, including lower rates of employ-ment that eventually lead to lower retirement savings, develop during adulthood. For instance, about 75 percent of men and 60 percent of women who were never poor as children were consistently employed as adults; only 34 percent of men and 28 percent of women who were poor for over half their childhood were consistently employed as adults (Ratcliffe and McKernan 2010).

One of the reasons for the effect of childhood poverty on financial resources is educational differences. Children in more affluent neighborhoods have access to better-funded public schools or, in some cases, to private schools. Differences in access to educational attainment have lasting effects on later employment and retirement income. By retirement, one 2009 analysis of the Current Population Survey data found that older Americans with only a high school diploma received $16,733 per year compared to $34,031 among college graduates (Purcell 2009). People with more education generally earn higher wages, and workers with less education are less consis-tently employed. This is particularly true of racial and ethnic minorities. Blacks with less than a high school education are employed just 47 percent of their young- to middle-working years on average (from age 18 to 44), compared to 68 percent for blacks with a high school education. In comparison, whites without a high school diploma are employed 64 percent of their adult working years, and whites with a high school diploma were employed 80 percent of the time (Bureau of Labor Statistics 2010b). Education has different effects across race and gender lines. As shown in Table 2.1, men earn more per week than women with comparable education. The median earnings for a man with a bachelor's degree were $1,199 per week in 2011, compared to $930 for a woman with comparable education.

Another potential reason for the persistence of poverty through the life course is the financial education that children do (or do not) receive through their home environments. Empirical research on **assets** and income has consistently shown that the wealth differential between white and minority households is much larger than the income differential. While lower rates of intergenerational transfers among minorities

Table 2.1 Median Weekly Earnings of People Aged 25 and Older by Education and Gender

	Less than a high school education	High school graduates, no college	Some college or associates degree	Bachelor's degree only	Advanced degree
Women	399	572	660	935	1145
Men	515	742	876	1254	1640

Source: Bureau of Labor Statistics 2012a

and barriers to accumulation of assets may play a role, part of the difference may stem from the less savings behavior and lower rates of return on assets (Choudhury 2001/2002). The economic environment of a person's childhood home may influence their later attitude toward savings and investments (Chiteji and Stafford 1999).

Benefits: The Role of Pension Wealth

The amount and types of employee benefits that workers receive, and the extent to which they take advantage of these benefits, is an important dimension of inequality. Benefits accounted for 31 percent of compensation for the average worker in 2012 (Bureau of Labor Statistics 2012b), so the gap between the compensation of low-wage workers without benefits and high-wage workers with benefits is larger than their wages alone would suggest. Disadvantaged workers are less likely to receive the job benefits that would help reduce financial risks. For instance, in 2011 only one in five low-wage workers had access to paid sick days (Gould 2011); they stood to lose more financially from sickness than higher-wage workers. The availability of sick days and paid vacation time play a role in preventing lower-wage workers from accumulating substantial amounts of retirement wealth.

Because of differential access to pension programs, inequality in wages translates into inadequate retirement savings for lower-wage workers. The highest-wage workers (those in the top 10 percent of the wage distribution) are much more likely to have access to pension programs through their employers than are the lowest-wage workers (those in the bottom 10 percent of the wage distribution). Beyond this surface discrepancy, the types of pensions, participation rates, and relatively generosity of pension program rules magnify the effects of low earnings on how much people save through pension plans. Although people of all wages are more likely to have access to defined-contribution pension plans than to have defined-benefit pension plans, the gap between the availability of the two pension types is widest among the lowest-wage workers. In 2009, 31 percent of workers in the lowest 10 percent of the wage distribution had access to defined-contribution pension plans, but only 6 percent of them had access to defined-benefit pension plans. Lower-wage workers tend not to participate in these plans at the same rate as higher-wage workers. In part, this may be due to the costs of participation, since employee contributions are typically required.

Some defined-contribution pension plans include an employer contribution without a matching contribution by employees, but these are concentrated among higher-wage workers (Bureau of Labor Statistics 2010d). Among lower-wage workers, the immediate need for income may discourage participation in pension plans (Muller, Moore, and Elliott 2009). Employer enrollment practices exacerbate the discrepancies in participation. While about 21 percent of high-wage workers (defined as those in the top 25 percent of the wage distribution) were automatically enrolled in their companies' retirement savings plan in 2010, it was much less common for workers near the bottom of the wage distribution to be automatically enrolled (Celis 2010). Even if they do choose to contribute, the percentage of their income that they contribute to their pension is likely to be lower. A 2006 analysis, for instance, found that less than 1 percent of workers who earned $40,000 to $60,000 a year contributed the maximum amount to their 401K plans (a type of defined contribution pension plan established by subsection 401(k) of the United States Internal Revenue Code), compared to 58 percent of those who earned $100,000 or more (Munnell and Sundén 2006). Due to the differences in the availability of employer pension programs, as well as the lower participation rates of low-wage workers, many reach retirement age with little pension wealth.

Interrupted Labor Force Participation

Many people do not work continuously during their pre-retirement years. For instance, some people take time off work for education. Other workers, particularly women, take time off full-time employment to raise children or provide elder care. All interruptions in labor force participation have the potential to reduce people's eventual retirement wealth, due to income not earned during time off from the labor force. However, unplanned interruptions are generally the most dangerous to a worker's later financial status. When labor force participation is interrupted for workers near the bottom of the occupational distribution, the consequences for them can be dire. Those with lower education and lower incomes are unlikely to receive severance benefits from their former employers because of the nature of their jobs (Heidkamp and Van Horn 2008). Further, re-employment can be a challenge. Focusing only on workers who had worked for the same employer for three or more years, one analysis found that more than half (51 percent) of the workers displaced from their jobs in 2007 and 2008 had not found new employment by January 2010 (Bureau of Labor Statistics 2010e).

Conclusion

This chapter discussed how inequalities develop from childhood until old age, within the framework of cumulative inequality. While some people are healthy enough to work, others are in relatively poor health. While some people can afford to retire, others lack retirement savings. Further, the older adults most in need of additional income are often those with the highest rates of disability (Johnson, Favreault, and Mommaerts, 2009). The idea of cumulative inequality provides a framework for understanding why certain people reach retirement age able to work or retire, while others do not. While this chapter discusses how inequality accumulates before the retirement years, the next chapter looks at how inequalities operate *during* the years at which most workers are approaching the typical retirement age.

DISCUSSION QUESTIONS

1. In this chapter we explore how cumulative inequality with respect to health and wealth takes place across the life course. Are there other such sources of cumulative inequality that may have implications for the employment prospects for older adults? For example, how about the cumulative nature of a person's social networks and contacts (sometimes referred to as "**social capital**")?

2. When you look at the community in which you grew up, based on what you observed over the years in that community, do you feel that the evidence does or does not seem to support the idea of "cumulative inequality" with respect to health and wealth discussed in this chapter?

III: Good Jobs: Unequal Access to Employment in Later Life

Some people enter the typical retirement years in good health and with money to spare. Others are in health too poor to continue to work comfortably in their current jobs, yet cannot afford to retire. Not every older adult who wants or needs to continue to work will be able to find suitable employment. From 2007 to 2009, the percentage of workers who planned to work in retirement increased from 63 percent to 72 percent (Helman, et al. 2009). However, while some people who expect not to work in retirement end up working for pay, it is much more common for the opposite to occur. People often think they will work in retirement, but then find that they cannot due to their health or because they cannot find a job (Maestas 2007). The gap between expectations about continued work and the reality that workers encounter is attributable to a range of factors, not the least of which is the lack of available jobs.

The issue of "good jobs" is particularly important to those at the bottom of the wage distribution. To some extent, the adversities that low-wage older workers face are shared by low-wage workers of various ages. Notably, in addition to declining average **real wages**—wages adjusted for inflation—recent decades have been characterized by increasing wage inequality (Autor, Katz, and Kearney 2008). However, the declines in health that older adults may experience further complicate their employment prospects. Much more than younger adults, older adults near the bottom of the wage distribution will find their employment opportunities limited by declining health.

In this chapter, we discuss the availability of jobs on two levels. First, we look at unequal access to *any* job, with a focus on **involuntary retirement**, **ageism**, and the role of health in limiting the type of jobs that people can get. On the most basic level, those who truly cannot afford to retire may need the income from any job, no matter how poorly paid or physically demanding. Second, we look at unequal access to *good* jobs, in terms of monetary compensation (e.g., wages and benefits) and the presence of employer policies that would make continued employment attractive to older workers. While many workers cannot afford to retire at their current standard of living, they may not necessarily opt for continued employment if the job is unacceptable to them.

Unequal Access to Jobs

How much access do older workers have to jobs? Are there more unemployed older workers than younger workers? This is a difficult question to answer in part because

Table 3.1 Unemployment Rates of Americans Aged 55 and Older

	2001	2002	2003	2004	2005	2006	2007	2008	2009	2010	2011
White men	3.1	3.8	4.1	3.7	3	2.8	3.1	3.6	6.7	7.3	6.5
Black men	4.6	5.9	6.6	6	6.2	5.5	5.1	7.6	10.2	11.9	11.8
White women	2.6	3.3	3.4	3.4	3	2.8	2.9	3.5	5.9	6	5.9
Black women	3.4	5.1	5.8	5.8	5.5	3.9	3.7	5.4	7	7.7	7.6

Source: Based on the 2001–2011 Current Population Survey

older workers who are unable to find work for a prolonged period of time often stop looking, becoming involuntarily retired. Although **unemployment rates**—the percentages of populations that are not employed and are looking for work—almost certainly underestimate the true level of unemployment among older workers, they provide some insight into which types of older workers have the most difficulty finding new jobs. Table 3.1, for instance, shows the unemployment rates for workers aged 55 and older, from 2001 to 2011. Even when the unemployment rate is relatively low, whites are substantially less likely to be unemployed than blacks. When the unemployment rate rises, the race differences are stark. For instance, in 2011, 6.5 percent of white men and 11.8 percent of black men were unemployed. These figures suggest that access to jobs (even counting those jobs that are not very desirable in terms of wages and benefits) is unequally distributed among older adults. In this section, we address the issue of unequal access to jobs, discussing (1) the concept of involuntary retirement, (2) the limiting effect of health, and (3) the role of age stereotypes.

Retired or Unemployed: The Role of Involuntary Retirement

If you lost your job, how long would you look for a new job before giving up? Most young and middle-aged adults, especially men, would continue looking for work indefinitely. With some exceptions, such as full-time homemakers (of which the majority are women), there is a social stigma attached to choosing not to work for younger and midlife workers. Further, people within this age range usually do not have substantial financial resources independent of paid employment. Deciding to exit the labor force is neither socially accepted nor financially possible for most of them. However, because retirement is an expected part of the life course, there is no stigma attached to leaving the labor force for older workers. Even a modest amount of retirement income, such as Social Security income, can make retirement more appealing than a fruitless job search. Consequently, older workers who are unemployed for a long period of time often "retire" because they cannot find jobs.

One analysis looked at workers aged 20 and older who were **displaced** from their jobs from 2007 to 2009. All of the workers studied had been employed by those organizations for at least three years. They lost their jobs due to factors such as plant closures, insufficient work, or elimination of positions, rather than because they quit their jobs or were fired. By January 2010, about 49 percent of them were re-employed, but only 15 percent had left the labor force. The remainder continued searching for employment. However, among displaced workers aged 65 and older, only 23 percent had found new employment. Most of the older workers who were not re-employed (45 percent of the displaced sample) had left the labor force rather than continuing to look for work (Bureau of Labor Statistics 2010e). When older workers become unemployed, they are significantly less likely than their younger counterparts to become re-employed (Johnson and Mommaerts 2011). Some researchers have estimated that about one in three people who retire in their fifties and sixties do so involuntarily, often because of business closures or layoffs (Johnson, Kawachi, and Lewis 2009). In 2010, almost 70 percent of unemployed workers aged 55 and older had stopped looking for work due to discouragement, compared to about 33 percent of those under the age of 55 (Heidkamp, Corre, and Van Horn 2010).

Involuntary retirement is not evenly distributed. Older workers in certain occupations and industries are more likely to retire if displaced from their jobs, because their skills are suited to shrinking niches. About 14 percent of older construction workers and 11 percent of older manufacturing workers were unemployed in 2009. Because of the conditions within the construction and manufacturing industries, these workers are less likely to find jobs in their previous occupations and may retire instead of changing occupations or remaining unemployed.

The dynamics of job loss also differ across ethnic groups and genders. One study found that job loss among Hispanics aged 45 and older was approximately double that of the population as a whole (Perron 2010). The question of job loss, unemployment, and retirement is particularly complicated by the fact that older minorities are less likely than older whites to identify themselves as retired when unemployed. Because their work histories are less likely to be continuous throughout the life course, minority workers tend not to see unemployment during their fifties and sixties as "retirement" to the same extent that workers with continuous work histories would (Gibson 1987). Further, older women have a greater tendency to retire when unemployed as compared to older men. Fifty-five percent of women aged 65 and older who were displaced from their jobs left the labor force (Bureau of Labor Statistics 2010e). Some of the cultural expectations of women—such as the role of homemaker, mother, and caregiver—are not strongly tied to paid employment, making an exit from the labor force more attractive to them when job options are limited.

Health and the Ability to Work

While many workers who retire involuntarily do so because they cannot find jobs, health plays a role in involuntary retirement as well. It is relatively uncommon for older workers to be *unable* to work due to their health. Only 8 percent of workers in their late sixties say that they are completely unable to work due to health problems (Adams, Dey, and Vickerie 2007). However, while the majority of older adults are healthy enough to work, they may not be healthy enough to work in the jobs that they can get. For instance, jobs might be available in janitorial work, but older adults who have health problems preventing them from lifting heavy loads cannot do these jobs. Similarly, retail jobs, where the worker is on his or her feet for long hours, might prove challenging for workers with mild movement impairments. For many older workers, the types of jobs that they have held in the past may no longer be available to them due to declining health. There is evidence that many newly created jobs will be in less physically demanding industries and occupations. For instance, 47 percent of job growth expected between now and 2018 will be in social sector jobs, such as government agencies (Bluestone and Melnick 2010), which generally require less physical activity than sectors such as manufacturing, which are projected to decrease in overall employment. However, not all older workers have the skills applicable to these jobs. If their skill set and work experience are not easily transferrable to less physically demanding jobs, they may not be able to find suitable employment. Consequently, a substantial minority of older adults stop working because their health prevents them from performing the jobs for which they are qualified, even if they can work in jobs with lower demands. For instance, in 2004, about one in three retirees aged 55 to 64 said that health problems were the primary reason they were not working (Dalirazar 2007). The gap between people who cannot work at all (less than one in 10) and those who stop working due to health (about one in three) is attributable partly to the physical demands of some jobs.

White-collar workers are much less likely to retire due to their health than blue-collar workers. Many of the health problems that are more common among older adults are more likely to affect workers in jobs with high physical requirements. For instance, compared to white-collar workers, blue-collar workers are much more likely to retire if they develop arthritis (Caban-Martinez, et al. 2011). A 2010 analysis of job characteristics found that about 35 percent of workers aged 58 and older were in physically demanding jobs (i.e., jobs that required substantial amounts of time standing, walking, or running, or making repetitive motions). Some of the most physically demanding jobs in which older workers were concentrated included cleaning (e.g., janitorial and housekeeping work), carpentry, and construction. These workers tended to have less education and to receive lower wages as compared to workers in less physically demanding jobs. For example, only 17 percent of workers in the top wage quintile (i.e., the higher 20 percent) had physically demanding jobs, compared to 56 percent of workers in the bottom wage quintile (i.e., the lowest 20 percent) (Rho 2010). Because workers near the bottom of the wage distribution tend to have poorer health and more demanding jobs, they are likely to involuntarily retire even when they cannot afford to do so.

Age Discrimination

At least as perceived by older workers, ageism and discrimination are major barriers to finding new employment. In 2009, almost one in four claims filed with the

United States Equal Employment Opportunity Commission focused on age discrimination, rather than other types of discrimination such as race or sex (U.S. Equal Employment Opportunity Commission 2010). Many unemployed older adults believe that they have not found a job because employers do not want to hire someone their age (MetLife 2009a). And, older adults who are employed sometimes believe that they are treated unfairly relative to younger workers in decisions about hiring, training, promotion, and raises (Groeneman 2008). For instance, in a 2005 survey, older workers said that they were treated unfairly relative to younger workers in a range of workplace decisions, such as hiring (44 percent), salary increases (32 percent), and promotions (25 percent) (Reynolds, Ridley, and Van Horn 2005).

Are older workers overstating the importance of age discrimination in preventing them from getting jobs? While claims of age discrimination may be exaggerated in some cases, there is evidence that it plays a role in keeping older workers from finding the right jobs or being treated fairly in the workplace. In a 2005 experiment, 4,000 pairs of fictional women's resumés (representing a younger woman, age 35 to 45, and an older woman, age 50 to 62) were sent to employers, and the younger woman's resumé was 42 to 46 percent more likely to be offered an interview than the older woman's resumé was—even when all other characteristics were the same (Lahey 2005). Other data indicates that older workers who lose their jobs are much less likely to become re-employed than younger workers who are otherwise identical. Men aged 50 to 61 who were displaced from their jobs were 39 percent less likely each month to become re-employed than men aged 25 to 34 (Johnson and Mommaerts 2011). While some of the perceived effects of discrimination may be due to age bias (e.g., "Older workers are stuck in their ways"), the costs of older workers in terms of health insurance and other benefits may also play a role. Regardless, whether because of poorer health or discrimination, older workers may not always be able to continue to work due to scarce employment opportunities.

Unequal Access to Good Jobs

Whether a worker can find a job—any job—is only part of the picture. What if the job involves hazardous conditions? What if it involves stressful working conditions? What if it pays too poorly to have any real effect on the workers' financial resources? Even if older workers can find jobs, it does not guarantee that those jobs will be good ones. In this section, we discuss two aspects of "good jobs" that go beyond the basics. First, we discuss the role of wage rates and hours worked. While workers may accept low-paying jobs or part-time jobs, they would often prefer a higher-paying full-time job. Second, we highlight the role of employer policies and programs, such as **phased retirement**, that might help older workers to work longer while easing into retirement. These aspects of a "good job" are unequally distributed across occupations, gender, ethnicities, and other categories.

Workers often have to leave the jobs at which they have worked, either due to economic circumstances or because their health no longer allows them to do the original job. When they do, there is abundant evidence that their new jobs will seldom be an improvement. Instead, new jobs tend to have poorer pay, inadequate benefits, and a tendency not to use the skills they have accumulated. One analysis of the Health and Retirement Study data found that when older workers (aged 45 to 75) changed jobs, their average hourly wages dropped by over $2 an hour (i.e., $18.57 to $16.23) (Johnson and Kawachi 2007). On average, men aged 25 to 34 earned 20 cents less per hour, men aged 35 to 49 earned 70 cents less per hour, men aged 50 to 61 earned $3.80 less per hour, and men aged 62 and older earned $5.70 less per hour on their new jobs, as compared to the jobs from which they were displaced (Johnson and Mommaerts 2011).

In part, the pay discrepancy may be due to the fact that many older workers have longer tenure (and hence higher pay) on their previous jobs. However, at least part of the difference is attributable to older workers who, either by necessity or choice, change occupations when they change jobs. In the most extreme cases, their previous experience and work history is rendered void, and the older worker starts out at the bottom of the wage ladder again. One study found that 27 percent of older workers who changed jobs switched occupations in the process, and the hourly wages in those new careers were substantially lower. Median wages for retirees in new jobs fell by 57 percent (Johnson, Kawachi, and Lewis 2009).

New jobs tend to be less financially desirable in other ways as well. They often do not have health insurance, pension plans, or even full-time hours. About a quarter of career changers lost their health insurance when moving to a new job but only one in 10 of them gained health insurance. For those older workers (51 and older) who switch careers, 61 percent said that their former employers provided pension plans, compared to only 20 percent of their new employers (Johnson, Kawachi, and Lewis 2009). Further, many older workers are employed in part-time jobs because full-time jobs are not available. In 2011, 17 percent of part-time workers aged 55 and older would have preferred to work full-time, but worked in part-time positions due to inadequate work or business conditions (GAO 2011). Rates of **underemployment** (employment situations that are subpar relative to the standard, typically in hours) are higher among women. For workers aged 60 to 64, 17 percent of women and 12 percent of men are underemployed (Slack and Jensen 2008). Hence, even among those who find jobs, older workers often are in jobs that pay lower wages and provide fewer benefits than their previous jobs.

Employer Policies: Beyond Wages and Benefits

Given the negative effects of job switches among older adults, some older adults might want to continue working for their current employer, but on different terms than standard full-time 9 to 5 jobs. Many recent retirees believe that, if they had been able to work seasonally, on a contract basis, or part-time, it would have encouraged them to delay their retirement (Helman, et al. 2008). However, most older workers do not have opportunities to remain employed for their organization on more flexible terms, and those that do are often higher-wage and more educated workers (Swanberg, Pitt-Catsouphes, and Drescher-Burke 2005), or in managerial roles (Yang and Reid 2006).

Workers at the top of the occupational hierarchy have the most access to the **flexible work options** (e.g., scheduling flexibility) (Golden 2009) that would allow them to informally phase into retirement in lieu of a formal phased retirement program. Further, the more secure that a worker's status is within their organization, the more likely they are to use the programs that are available. Even if an organization institutes flexible work options, individual workers may not have practical access to these options. Organizations sometimes adopt policies and programs for symbolic reasons, such as to show that they are socially responsible employers (Powell and DiMaggio 1991), without fully committing to making those programs available to their entire workforce. When key groups within organizations, such as supervisors, have little stake in implementing the policies, extremely small numbers of workers may actually have access (Eaton 2003). Supervisors may not make options available to all of their employees (Thompson, Beauvais, and Lyness 1999), or workers may fear that using these options will endanger their jobs indirectly (Eaton 2003). For instance, workers might wonder if taking advantage of a phased retirement program or transferring to a job with less responsibility would cause their supervisors to view them as less committed to the organization. In one 2002 survey, 79 percent of employees surveyed said that they would want to use flexible work options if there were no negative consequences at work (Galinsky, Bond, and Hill 2004).

Programs specifically geared to encouraging continued labor force participation among older adults—such as job sharing, phased retirement, and career on-ramps and off-ramps (employer policies or job positions that help workers to leave career jobs or re-enter the workforce after a break)—are among the least prevalent of flexibility policies (WorldatWork 2011). While many organizations say that they allow at least some workers to phase into retirement, only about 6 percent of employers offer formal phased retirement programs (Society for Human Resource Management 2010). Formal phased retirement programs are very rare in part because of regulatory and legal barriers (Hewitt Associates 2008). According to a 2009 survey of large employers, most employers believe that regulatory complexities, tax issues, age discrimination laws, and a host of other barriers prevent formal phased retirement programs from being practical for them (MetLife 2009b).

Despite these barriers, many employers offer phased retirement to a minority of their workforce, even if informally. For example, about half of the employers who responded to a 2005 survey said that they allowed at least *some* employees to phase into retirement, but almost none provided this option for all their older employees (Bond, T. J. et al. 2005). Typically, only the most affluent workers are in a position to use phased retirement programs because these programs often involve the loss of pension plans and health insurance. In one 2003 survey of 500 employers, 26 percent of employers said that the health insurance benefits of workers who phased into retirement were not adversely affected (Hutchens 2003). Even among white-collar workers, fewer than 10 percent were able to phase into retirement in an advantageous manner. Instead, most employees would need to give up or change their health insurance, move to a different job, or be rehired as a new employee or at lesser pay as part of phasing into retirement (Hutchens and Chen 2006).

Conclusion

Access to jobs—and specifically to *good* jobs—is unequally distributed. Many older adults involuntarily retire because they cannot find suitable employment. However, even among those who find jobs, those jobs may offer low financial compensation (due to low wage rates per hour and/or insufficient number of hours worked) or lack the programs (such as phased retirement policies) that would encourage older adults to stay employed. Because of these factors, older adults who work tend to fall into two categories: a relatively advantaged group that *wants* to work and a relatively disadvantaged group that *needs* to work. For instance, one 2007 study examined the chances that older adults would move into new jobs after retiring from their main careers. Among those born from 1942 to 1947, the people most likely to work in post-career jobs were those who had earned the highest wages during their career jobs and those who had earned the lowest wages (Giandrea, Cahill, and Quinn 2007). Those who want to work are often the small minority that have access—formally or informally—to employer policies and benefits that make continued work possible and enjoyable. Those who need to work may continue to work, if they can find employment, despite the fact that the jobs available to them may not be good ones.

DISCUSSION QUESTIONS

1. In this chapter one of the topics discussed is unequal access to good jobs. It is safe to assume that the attributes associated with what it means to be in a "good job" differ from one worker to another. How might the attributes most often mentioned differ for workers in different age ranges? For example, in their early twenties, late thirties, late sixties, and mid-seventies?
2. In this chapter we discuss the issue of unequal access to jobs for different categories of workers. Are there other important categories of workers that we did not mention?

IV: Unintended Consequences: How Would Working Longer Change Our Lives?

Encouraging or expecting people to work longer might help us to better adapt to the potential financial burdens of an aging society. In addition to increasing funding to entitlement programs such as Social Security, longer working lives would ideally decrease poverty among older adults whose retirement income falls short of the standard of living acceptable to them. It might also ease the burden on families who provide financial assistance to elders. Today, about one in four workers aged 50 and older provide financial assistance to their parents or in-laws (MetLife 2011), and many others worry that they will come under pressure to provide financially for elderly relatives but be unable to do so (MetLife 2009c).

We have already noted that the potential effects of working longer are unlikely to be evenly distributed across different segments of the population defined by race, ethnicity, gender, and socioeconomic status. In part because of these differences, extended labor force participation might also have a number of **unintended consequences**. Unintended consequences are the effects of social actions that fall outside of their original purpose. The intended consequences of encouraging later labor force participation are primarily financial, both at the societal (e.g., entitlement program funding) and individual (i.e., increased income for older adults) levels. The unintended consequences, however, would likely extend far beyond these financial considerations. While it is difficult to anticipate all the consequences of a wide-ranging social change such as extended labor force participation, existing research suggests some potential results, both positive and negative. How would our lives change if we were all expected to work longer?

In the Workplace

If older adults worked longer, the average age of workers in most organizations would increase. Additionally, the age diversity of the workplace would increase. People might regularly have co-workers half a century older or younger than themselves. Potential unintended consequences of these changes include: (1) effects of age diversity, (2) ageism or **reverse ageism**, and (3) skill shortages and training issues.

How could changing age demographics shape how people relate to other people in the workplace? Would it lead to more conflict, or less? There are at least three mechanisms through which "working longer" could change workplace dynamics, and it is not obvious whether the changing age demographics would lead to workplaces that function better, worse, or just differently.

First, there is evidence that people tend to identify with co-workers whom they perceive as similar to themselves. That is, "Birds of a feather flock together." Often, particularly when co-worker relationships are relatively new, people are perceived as similar if they are the same race, ethnicity, gender, or age. For instance, two women of around the same age might assume that they share underlying similarities, even if actual similarities in outlook are very superficial. Demographic similarities within work groups have generally been found to reduce levels of conflict and to increase levels of teamwork, particularly among workers with low tenure. In particular, similarities in race (Avery, McKay, and Wilson 2008; Avey, West, and Crossley 2008; Stewart and Garcia-Prieto 2008) and gender (Choi 2007) can act as launching places for people to begin working together effectively. From this perspective, the idea of people working longer would seem worrisome because the more age-diverse the workplace becomes, the fewer similarities there may be to tie people together. However, it is not a foregone conclusion that an age-diverse workplace will be one of increasing conflict. There is some evidence that age may be an exception to the idea that people of similar characteristics always bond together. People have lifelong exposure to different ages, so that they can more easily communicate with someone of a different age than with someone of a different race (Goldberg 2005).

Second, if the workforce ages rapidly, **organizational timetables** (i.e., the organizational beliefs about when a worker receives certain promotions or moves into certain types of jobs) may come into conflict with demographic realities. In the United States, despite the increasing number of people who begin or switch careers in mid- to late life, expectations about when a worker receives promotions are linked to their age (Lashbrook 1995). One study of three workplaces found that if workers did not reach the expected level in the organizational hierarchy (such as a promotion to a senior or management position) within the normative timeframe, they received lower performance ratings (Lawrence 1995). How will organizational timetables be affected if more older workers choose to remain in the labor force, even if they move to new organizations or occupations, starting new careers?

Third, diversity in age might make teams more rather than less effective. The more diverse a group is, the more varied their range of knowledge; a team made up of workers of all different ages may have a synergy that a group made up of all younger or all older workers would not (Choi 2007). Age diversity might lead to lower emotional conflict within teams (Pelled, Eisenhardt, and Xin 1999), because workers of the same age may be more likely to develop competitive co-worker relationships, leading to escalating conflict, whereas workers of all different ages might be more likely to form mentoring relationships.

Current knowledge on age diversity suggests that diversity in age is not necessarily bad for workplaces, but the way that individuals, work groups, and organizations react to that diversity often is. One of the major factors underlying whether diversity in general leads to positive or negative outcomes is supervisor or manager skill in dealing with complex, diverse teams. Managers can help identify problems related to know-ledge-sharing and trust, heading off problems caused by the perceived dissimilarities between workers (Gratton, Voight, and Erickson 2007). They can also promote group inclusion by developing a strong relationship with each member of the work group (Nishii and Mayer 2009). In a best-case scenario, a skilled supervisor could turn increased age diversity into an important business asset. Whether supervisors and organizations will have the skills to manage an age-diverse workplace is an open ques-tion. The more rapidly the workforce ages, the more rapid organizational response will need to be to effectively adjust.

Ageism and Reverse Ageism in the Workplace

In Chapter 3, we discussed the ageism that older workers encounter. However, if the workforce ages, would younger workers find themselves at a disadvantage as a result of reverse ageism—stereotypes directed against younger workers, as opposed to older workers? Currently, legislation for sex, race, national origin, and religion protects *both* the majority (e.g., white) and minority (e.g., black) groups. The same is not true of legislation directed toward age discrimination. Under federal law, organizations can favor an older individual at the expense of a younger individual because of age, but the opposite (i.e., favoring a younger individual because of age) is illegal (Code of Federal Regulations, Title 29).

In part, reverse ageism may occur as a result of the differences in what generations expect of one another in the workplace. Surveys show that workers from the earlier generations are more likely to consider being ethical and professional as extremely or very important to the workplace, as compared to workers from Generation Y (also known as "the Millenials," following Generation X – the generation born after the baby boom generation) (Ranstad Work Solutions 2007), and that people of all ages generally believe that older generations have better work ethics (Taylor and Morin 2009; Pew Research Center 2010). To the extent that older generations have different definitions of what is acceptable professional behavior, younger workers may find themselves at a disadvantage in hiring and promotion decisions. For instance, younger workers may be passed over for promotion to supervisory positions or be considered unsuited to supervisory roles, as people expect supervisors to be older than themselves (Collins, Hair, and Rocco 2009).

Older adults might also indirectly affect the career prospects of younger workers, simply because the older worker would fill their jobs longer. Historically, when women entered the labor force during and after World War II, it did not have adverse effects on the job prospects of men, but the aging workforce might differ in two important ways. First, while women tended to work in different occupations than men, older and younger workers might occupy the same range of jobs. For example, workers under the age of 25 represent about half of those paid the Federal minimum wage or less (Bureau of Labor Statistics 2010a) and older workers, specifically those over 65, are also disproportionately likely to be in low-wage jobs (GAO 2011). Second, the period after World War II was characterized by extensive economic growth; to the extent that this is no longer true, a sufficient number of new jobs may not be generated for older and younger workers who want or need to work.

Further, **reverse institutional ageism**, unfair treatment of younger workers embedded within organizational rules and practices, might result from organizational decisions related to the aging workforce. For instance, older workers are more costly than younger workers (Munnell, Sass, and Soto 2006), because of higher earnings (Adler and Hilber 2009) and the costs of benefits such as paid time off (Towers Perrin 2005). A major source of the costs of older workers is health insurance. Insurance claim costs for workers aged 20 to 24 are about 60 percent lower than for workers aged 55 to 64 for indemnity and 40 percent lower for medical costs. In part, this is because older workers generally receive more treatments than younger workers (Restrepo, Sobel, and Shuford 2006) and need more days of recuperation when they are hurt (Bureau of Labor Statistics 2009). Potentially, organizations could scale back insurance for all employees to control the costs involved in employing a higher number of older workers. While this would still provide older workers with more adequate health insurance than they would receive if they did not work at all, it would adversely affect the health insurance available to younger workers. Another path would be to offer better or different health insurance to older workers, as compared to younger workers, in order to control costs. Because the ADEA specifically focuses on workers aged 40 and older, younger workers might have more difficulty obtaining legal recourse against reverse ageism.

Help Wanted: Skill Shortages and Training

As the workforce ages, will some skills be in short supply? Current research suggests that older adults may be less comfortable than members of Generation Y when dealing with people of different ethnicities, cultures, and sexual orientations (Hewlett, et al. 2009; Taylor and Morin 2009). There is evidence that older adults are less comfortable than younger adults using the Internet and other technologies. About two in five older adults (aged 50 and older) consider themselves very or extremely comfortable using the Internet, but this is not equally true across racial and ethnic minorities. Only one in five Hispanic older adults consider themselves very or extremely comfortable using the Internet (Koppen 2010). Only about one-quarter of white older adults say that they have difficulty keeping up with technologies (Groeneman 2008), compared to 46 percent of Hispanics and 31 percent of blacks.

In the context of an aging population, training and education to develop new skills is likely to be increasingly important for both employers and employees. Lifetime employment is an unrealistic expectation for almost all employee–employer relationships today. In fact, job security has eroded to the point where many people do not know if they will be employed by their organization in the next week, month, or year. Hence, if more people work beyond their early sixties, their chances of working for a large number of different employers, occupations, and industries increase.

Job security was traditionally the cornerstone of the **psychological contract**— the implicit agreement about what constitutes a "fair" exchange between employees and employers. That is, employees were committed to and engaged in their work partly because they believed their employers would provide steady employment and help in difficult times (Baruch 2001; Rousseau 1995). Today, businesses still need employees who go "above and beyond" to succeed in a competitive economy, but they cannot offer the same levels of job security. By providing employees with the skills and competencies that they would need to find new jobs, training may provide a working basis for a psychological contract in the absence of true job security (Benson 2006). Offering training and development opportunities to workers—most of whom expect to work for numerous employers over the course of their working lives— positively affects their attitudes toward and commitment to their organizations (Bartlett 2001; Galunic and Anderson 2000; Tanksy and Cohen 2001). Hence, the more working lives are extended, the more we might expect training to affect how well businesses function.

In light of the importance of training to maintaining the employability of workers, it is problematic that older workers typically receive less on-the-job training than younger workers (Eyster, et al. 2008; Sparrow and Davies 1988). In part, this reflects the higher costs of training older workers. Because their job tenure is higher, they tend to be more highly compensated per hour worked than younger workers are. Hence, providing training to them during normal working hours is— hour per hour—more costly to their employers. However, one of the major underlying reasons that older workers receive less training than younger workers may be outdated assumptions. That is, to the extent that older workers are expected to retire soon, employers anticipate fewer years during which they can personally reap the benefits of their training programs (Simpson, Greller, and Stroh 2002), making the perceived **return on investment** lower for older workers than for younger workers. However, due both to the lower average turnover of older employees (Swaen, et al. 2002) and the trend away from lifetime employment (Simpson, et al. 2002), older workers do not necessarily leave their organizations sooner than younger workers do.

Even if older workers begin to receive training and development at the same levels as their younger counterparts, however, human resource approaches to training may need to be adapted. Younger employees are typically near the beginning of their careers, when they are learning the basic skills and competencies needed in a particular organization, industry, or occupation. The more experience and knowledge that workers amass over their lifetimes, the less that "generic" training programs will benefit them. The skills that older employees need to develop may be unique, specific, and difficult to convey in generic training programs (Simpson, et al. 2002), requiring a rethinking of employee training programs to fully tap into the potential of an aging workforce.

Conversely, older workers would need to rethink the expectation of staying in the same occupation or industry over the course of their working lives. If older adults remained in the labor force longer, career changes might be viewed as the norm, rather than an exception. Older men change industries and occupations at comparable rates to younger workers when re-employed after being displaced from their original jobs. Among those aged 50 to 61, 49 percent of men displaced from their jobs and re-employed in new jobs are in new occupations. A total of 47 percent of men aged 62 and older and re-employed were in new occupations. These figures are comparable to re-employed men aged 25 to 34 (50 percent) and 35 to 49 (48 percent). However, only 38 percent of women over the age of 62 and re-employed were in new occupations, compared to 62 percent of women under the age of 25 (Johnson and Mommaerts 2011).

Effects on the Well-being of Older Adults

Financial effects aside, is retirement better or worse than work for the typical older adult? Today, the majority of retired workers say that they are happier in retirement than they were when working (Koppen and Anderson 2008). About three in four full-time retirees are very or pretty happy with their lives (Taylor, et al. 2009), and the vast majority of older adults who are out of the labor force say that they do not want to work for pay (97 percent) (Rix 2011). Among older grandparents, 31 percent of women and 19 percent of men said that what they valued most about aging was that they were able to spend time with their grandchildren (Livingston and Parker 2010), and to the extent that retirement opens up the possibilities of people engaging in new and meaningful opportunities, it can lead to better well-being and health. However, the preferences of people currently out of the labor force are only part of the picture. People may be satisfied with their lives in retirement in part because they have come to expect a declining investment in work as they age. While 5 percent of older adults (aged 50 or older) say that success in their career is one of their top dreams for the future, the remaining 95 percent focused on other dreams such as traveling and spending time with family members (AARP 2011). If people expected to work into their sixties or seventies, their goals might remain work-focused longer. Although the majority of workers who postpone retirement do so for financial reasons, only a small minority—about one in 10 according to one survey (Helman, Copeland, and VanDerhei 2011)—do not cite other reasons for working as well. Reasons might include enjoying their job, enjoying where they work, fearing boredom in retirement, and enjoying feeling needed (Careerbuilder 2011).

Given the importance of the current norms surrounding labor force participation in shaping whether older adults rate their subjective well-being more or less highly in retirement, it is far from certain what the effects of encouraging later labor force participation would be on the well-being of older adults if norms changed in the future. In this section, we draw on what is known about age, health, and social connectedness to explore some potential consequences of "working longer" for the well-being of older adults, including (1) health, (2) self-esteem, and (3) social connectedness.

Health: Does Working Longer Mean Better Health?

On the surface, it makes sense that older adults who remain in the labor force longer might better maintain their mental and physical health than those who retired. Medical research has long shown that physical activity promotes the well-being of older adults. For example, one study of older women found that women who walked regularly experienced less decline in their cognitive faculties over a period of eight years (Yaffe, et al. 2001). Other studies have pointed to the importance of strenuous physical activity in maintaining cognitive functioning (Albert, et al. 1995). The link between physical activity and health stems from a variety of factors, such as lower risks of coronary heart disease (National Institute of Health 1996). Logically, if retirees become more sedentary, their health may deteriorate. Despite this, there is little evidence that delaying retirement leads to better health for the majority of workers. Some studies have found that continued work leads to better health, while others have found that it leads to worse health. For instance, one study of older adults found that, once the effect of health on retirement had been taken into account (i.e., people in poor health are more likely to retire), retirement tends to prevent deterioration in people's self-rated health. Older adults who retired were more likely than those who continued working to say that their health was about the same or better than it was two years in the past. However, when their health was measured using less subjective measures (e.g., whether they had various functional limitations), retirement had little to no effect (Neuman 2008). Other studies have found similarly complex—and seemingly contradictory—results (Rijs, Cozijnsen, and Deeg 2012).

In part, these apparent contradictions stem from the diverse employment situations of older adults. Whether someone is working or not is a comparatively unimportant factor in their physical and psychological well-being, relative to the specific conditions of work or retirement. For instance, physical activity promotes better health, but not all jobs include much physical activity and some jobs (e.g., clerical) might discourage strenuous physical activities. Some people become relatively sedentary and isolated in retirement, while others engage in **volunteering**, **caregiving**, travel, and hobbies.

Self-esteem: Do Retirees Lose Self-esteem?

How does retirement affect self-esteem? If people were expected to work longer, would their self-esteem suffer, or would they have better self-esteem due to continued work? There are two competing schools of thought for understanding the effects of retirement on self-esteem (Reitzes and Mutran 2006). First, following Miller (1965), some authors have argued that retirement, by taking the work role from people, would cause identity crises that would leave retirees without a solid sense of self-worth. Second, other research has followed Atchley's (1971) observation that most retired workers have continuity of family and other roles as they transition into retirement, minimizing the effect of retirement on self-esteem. Additionally, because retirement as a role includes numerous rights and expectations (e.g., a right to economic support through mechanisms such as Social Security), the work role is generally replaced with the retired role instead of leaving a void.

Most research on self-esteem and retirement in the past few decades has supported the idea that the retired role replaces the work role, confirming that retirement does not typically lead to lower self-esteem (Reitzes, Mutran, and Fernandez 1996). Although a person's response to retirement may evolve over time as retirees come to terms with the reality of everyday life in retirement (Atchley 1976), most people adjust to retirement relatively well because it is a normal and expected stage of life. This means that the effects of retirement on self-esteem for *current* retirees may be only part of the picture because so much is dependent on norms. If retirement were no longer *expected* for adults in their sixties, for instance, those who do have to stop working might experience declines in self-esteem.

Research on people who are "forced" to retire supports this perspective. Regardless of age, adults who are unemployed long-term say they have lost self-respect, suffered depression, and experienced strained family relations (Morin and Kochbar 2010). Hence, it is not surprising that many older unemployed job seekers suffer from strained family relations or avoid social situations as a result of not being able to find a job (Heidkamp, et al. 2010). While unemployment leads to lower self-esteem among people of all ages, older adults are more likely than younger adults to have health considerations that limit the amount and type of work they can do. Further, forced retirement may lead to negative effects throughout the retirement years; for instance, people who are forced to retire are more likely to experience declining health in retirement, as compared to those who choose to retire (Crowley 1986). Hence, social expectations encouraging older workers to work longer could indirectly damage their health and self-esteem in retirement, if opportunities to work (i.e., access to jobs) and ability to work (i.e., health) do not keep pace. Conversely, if most older adults can continue to work as long as social norms would suggest, encouraging later labor force participation would probably not have negative effects.

Social Connectedness: Are Retirees Less Connected?

Another potential concern is whether retirement, by taking people out of work-related networks, might lead to isolation and lack of social support. Social networks (i.e., the set of contacts to whom people are connected) of older adults are smaller than those of younger and middle-aged adults (Ajrouch, Blandon, and Antonucci 2005) and older adults have less contact with friends as they age (Shaw, et al. 2007). It is not clear how much of this effect is due to retirement itself. As health problems increase, older adults may be less able to maintain connections with other people if those connections require physical activities (Cornwell 2011). Further, as people age, they may simply become less interested in maintaining a wide range of contacts, preferring to focus on a smaller number of meaningful relationships (Carstensen, Isaacowitz, and Charles 1999).

How much of the declining network size of older adults is due to retirement, and how much is due to age itself? One 2011 study analyzed data on more than 92,000 Americans to evaluate the effects of various factors on how much contact individuals had with other people. The study concluded that the amount of social contact that people had with other people declined noticeably with age, and that a substantial portion of that decline was due to changes that tend to occur with age—such as changes in living arrangements and work—rather than to age itself. Employed people tended to have more nonwork social contact than the unemployed, but the pattern was less clear for retirement. Retired women reported more nonwork social exposure, while retired men reported less (Cornwell 2011). Hence, while employment may maintain certain social ties by requiring work-related contact, it is not a foregone conclusion that extended labor force participation would help older adults to maintain their networks and social contacts in nonwork-related arenas. Based on existing research, the effects of retirement on social connectedness would vary widely based on factors such as gender.

Effects on Family and Community

The consequences of working longer would extend beyond the workplace. In this section, we discuss three ways in which extended labor force participation among older adults might have unintended consequences on other aspects of our lives, including (1) caregiving and (2) volunteer-reliant organizations.

Caregiving

Expecting older adults to continue working longer may have unintentional effects on caregiving (i.e., unpaid help with basic needs and tasks). By some estimates, more than 90 percent of adults aged 50 and older provide informal help to their family and friends (Kahn, McGill, and Bianchi 2011). While younger and middle-aged caregivers often provide care for a parent or grandparent, caregivers over the typical age of retirement (i.e., 65) tend to care for spouses, siblings, or nonrelatives (National Alliance for Caregiving, AARP, and MetLife 2009). Additionally, a large amount of the caregiving provided by older adults is to grandchildren. In 2010, approximately 39 percent of grandparents had helped their adult children with child care within the past year (Livingston and Parker 2010).

If older adults were expected to work longer, would the amount of caregiving they could provide decrease? A substantial number of working caregivers would prefer to reduce their hours at work (Aumann, et al. 2010), suggesting that caregiving and working at the same time can create time pressures. Further, employed caregivers often say that they have gone in to work late, left early, or taken time off during the day due to their caregiving responsibilities (National Alliance for Caregiving, AARP, and MetLife 2009). However, the amount of caregiving provided by workers, as compared to those who are not working, is surprisingly equal. People who do not work are only slightly more likely to provide elder care than those who are employed, particularly among women (MetLife 2011). Caregiving responsibilities are rarely given as a reason for retiring (Parkinson 2002). While expecting continued labor force participation might affect the amount of time devoted to caregiving, existing research suggests that these effects would be slight. Instead, the bulk of the effect might be felt in the additional stress placed upon working caregivers.

Volunteering

What we know about volunteering behavior among older adults highlights how diversity translates into the retirement years. In general, people with more capital—such as human and social capital—are more likely to get involved in productive activities such as volunteering during their retirement years (Wilson and Musick 1997). People with more **human capital** (i.e., an individual's knowledge, skills, and abilities), such as education and health, are more likely to volunteer (Choi, et al. 2007; Wilson 2000). Perhaps this is because volunteer organizations, like employers, are likely to put the most effort into recruiting individuals with higher human capital (Verba, Schlozman, & Brady 1995). People with more social capital (i.e., the social linkages through which an individual may gain knowledge or resources) are also more likely to volunteer. The more social linkages people have, whether with family, friends, or neighbors, the more likely they are to be recruited into volunteer organizations. Even though the care of children requires a substantial time investment, having children is generally associated with higher volunteer involvement (Butrica, Johnson, and Zedlewski 2009). Parents have social linkages through school and youth activities that keep them plugged into volunteer organizations.

What we know about volunteering suggests that whether a person is employed, a parent, or a retiree matters less than the conditions of their job or retirement.

For instance, regarding employment, people who work relatively low numbers of hours may be recruited into volunteer organizations through their co-workers and have sufficient free time to volunteer often. However, older adults who work longer hours are less likely to volunteer due to competition for their time (Butrica, et al. 2009; Mutchler, Burr, and Caro 2003).

The conditions surrounding continued labor force participation would play a strong role in determining whether organizations that rely on volunteers would experience any labor shortages. The number of people volunteering might increase, but the number of high-commitment volunteers with managerial skills might decrease at certain volunteer organizations. Older adults are less likely to volunteer than adults at midlife. For instance, in 2010, about 24 percent of adults aged 65 and older volunteered at some point during the course of the year, compared to 32 percent of adults aged 35 to 44 years. Likewise, even controlling for factors such as health, older adults who become employed are more likely to volunteer than older adults who leave employment (Butrica, et al. 2009). Because older adults often hear about volunteering activities through their work acquaintances, having a network of co-workers can lead them to volunteering.

The tendency of younger, employed adults to be more likely to volunteer can mask the unique roles filled by older, retired volunteers. Older volunteers, particularly those who are not employed, average more hours a week than their younger counterparts. The median number of hours volunteered per year among adults aged 35 to 44 was 48, compared to 96 hours among adults aged 65 and older. The longer volunteering hours among older adults are largely driven by the fact that they are out of the labor force. The median number of hours volunteered among those out of the labor force was 72, compared to 48 for those in the labor force. Hence, while being employed pulls people into volunteering through work-related networks, employment also relates to lower numbers of hours volunteered because people who are employed typically have less time to volunteer.

Older volunteers typically fill different roles and volunteer at different types of organizations than younger volunteers. Volunteers at midlife, who often have children attending school, tend to volunteer through educational organizations. In 2010, about 40 percent of volunteers aged 35 to 44 were primarily involved in educational or youth service organizations. In comparison, only 9 percent of volunteers aged 65 and older were concentrated in this type of organization. Conversely, older adults disproportionately volunteer for religious organizations. In 2010, some 45 percent of volunteers aged 65 and older volunteered for religious organizations compared to 27 percent of those aged 35 to 44. Older adults are also more likely than their younger counterparts to volunteer in professional or managerial capacities, such as managing other volunteers or serving on committees. About 11 percent of volunteers aged 55 to 64 and 9 percent of volunteers aged 65 and older mainly performed professional or managerial tasks, compared to 7 percent of volunteers aged 35 to 44 (Bureau of Labor

Statistics 2011). Further, certain volunteering programs are heavily dependent on older adults, such as intergenerational tutoring programs, which have been shown to foster reading skills of children (Gattis, et al. 2010; Lee, et al. 2010).

If older adults were to work longer, we would not expect the number of people volunteering to decrease, but we might expect shortages in certain types of volunteers, including those able to devote relatively long hours, those with managerial or professional skills, and those volunteering through religious organizations.

Conclusion

How would working longer change our lives? This chapter has discussed some of the potential consequences of extended labor force participation, both in the workplace and beyond the workplace. At face value, it seems to make sense that if the average person *lives* longer and is *healthy* longer, they should *work* longer as well. But is "working longer" really the answer? The diversity among older adults—in race, ethnicity, gender, and socioeconomic status, as well as in health and wealth—makes the question of "working longer" particularly complex. While encouraging older adults to work past the typical age of retirement might have many benefits, particularly from the perspective of reducing the potential burden of an aging population, these benefits would come at a cost of unequal burdens for different groups of older adults. Like health, wealth, and access to good jobs, the unintended consequences of working longer—both good and bad—are likely to be unequally distributed across socio-economic, gender, race, and ethnic lines.

DISCUSSION QUESTIONS

1. In this chapter we have discussed a number of possible unintentional consequences of successful efforts to get older workers to work longer. What are some additional consequences that you can think of that would have consequences at the national or the state level?
2. We argued that the traditional psychological contract between employees and employers has eroded due to the lack of job security that most employers today can or will offer. Do you expect job security from your employer? If not, what do you expect?

References

AARP. 2011. "Voices of 50+ America: Dreams & Challenges." Washington, DC: AARP. Retrieved October 26, 2012 (http://assets.aarp.org/rgcenter/general/voices-america-dreams-challenges-national.pdf).

Adams, P. F., A. N. Dey, and J. L. Vickerie. 2007. "Summary Health Statistics for the U.S. Population: National Health Interview Survey, 2005. Vital and Health Statistics, Series 10." *Data from the National Health Survey 233*: 1–104.

Adler, G., and D. Hilber. 2009. "Industry Hiring Patterns of Older Workers." *Research on Aging 31*: 69–88. doi: 10.1177/0164027508324635.

Administration on Aging. 2010. "A Profile of Older Americans 2009." Washington, DC: U.S. Department of Health and Human Services. Retrieved October 26, 2012 (http://www.aoa.gov/AoARoot/Aging_Statistics/Profile/2009/docs/2009profile_508.pdf).

Age Discrimination in Employment Act of 1967, Pub. L. No. 90-202 Code, 29 U.S.C. § 621 through 29 U.S.C. § 634.

Ajrouch, K. K., A. Y. Blandon, and T. C. Antonucci. 2005. "Social Networks Among Men and Women: The Effects of Age and Socioeconomic Status." *Journal of Gerontology Series B: Psychological Sciences and Social Sciences 60B*: S311–17.

Albert, M. S., K. Jones, C. R. Savage, L. Berkman, T. Seeman, D. Blazer, and J. W. Rowe. 1995. "Predictors of Cognitive Change in Older Persons: MacArthur Studies of Successful Aging." *Psychology and Aging 10*: 578–89. doi: 10.1037//0882-7974.10.4.578.

Anguelov, C. E., and C. R. Tamborini. 2009. "Retiring in Debt? Differences between the 1995 and 2004 Near-retiree Cohorts." *Social Security Bulletin 69(2)*: 13–34. Retrieved October 26, 2012 (http://www.ssa.gov/policy/docs/ssb/v69n2/v69n2p13.html).

Arias, E. 2011. "United States Life Tables, 2007 (National Vital Statistics Reports No. 59-9)." Washington, DC: Centers for Disease Control and Prevention. Retrieved October 26, 2012 (http://www.cdc.gov/nchs/data/nvsr/nvsr59/nvsr59_09.pdf).

Atchley, R. C. 1971. "Retirement and Leisure Participation: Continuity or Crisis?" *The Gerontologist 11*: 3–17.

———. 1976. *The Sociology of Retirement.* New York: John Wiley and Sons.

Aumann, K., E. Galinsky, K. Sakai, M. Brown, and J. T. Bond. 2010. "The Elder Care Study: Everyday Realities and Wishes for Change." New York: Families and Work Institute. Retrieved October 26, 2012 (http://familiesandwork.org/site/research/reports/elder_care.pdf).

Autor, D. H., L. F. Katz, and M. S. Kearney. 2008. "Trends in U.S. Wage Inequality: Revising the Revisionists." *The Review of Economics and Statistics 90*: 300–23. doi: 10.1162/rest.90.2.300.

Avery, D. R., P. F. McKay, and D. C. Wilson. 2008. "What Are the Odds? How Demographic Similarity Affects the Prevalence of Perceived Employment Discrimination." *Journal of Applied Psychology 93*: 235–49. doi: 10.1037/0021-9010.93.2.235.

Avey, J. B., B. J. West, and C. D. Crossley. 2008. "The Association between Ethnic Congruence in the Supervisor–Subordinate Dyad and Subordinate Organizational Position and Salary." *Journal of Occupational and Organizational Psychology 81*: 551–66. doi: 10.1348/096317907X241588.

Bartlett, K. R. 2001. "The Relationship between Training and Organizational Commitment: A Study in the Health Care Field." *Human Resource Development Quarterly 12*: 335–53.

Baruch, Y. 2001. "Employability: A Substitute for Loyalty?" *Human Resource Development International* 4: 543–66.

Benson, G. S. 2006. "Employee Development, Commitment, and Intention to Turnover: A Test of Employability Policies in Action." *Human Resource Management Journal 16*: 173–92.

Bluestone, B., and M. Melnik 2010. "After the Recovery: Help Needed: The Coming Labor Shortage and How People in Encore Careers Can Help Solve It." United States: Civic Ventures and MetLife. Retrieved October 26, 2012 (http://www.encore.org/files/research/JobsBluestonePaper3-5-10. pdf).

Board of Trustees of the Federal Old-Age and Survivors Insurance and Federal Disability Insurance Trust Funds (Board of Trustees). 2011. *The 2011 Annual Report of the Board of Trustees of the Federal Old-Age and Survivors Insurance and Federal Disability Insurance Trust Funds.* Washington, DC: U.S. Government Printing Office.

Bond, T. J., E. Galinsky, S. S. Kim, and E. Brownfield. 2005. "2005 National Study of Employers." New York, NY: Families and Work Institute. Retrieved October 26, 2012 (http://familiesandwork. org/site/research/reports/2005nse.pdf).

Bond, J. T., E. Galinsky, M. Pitt-Catsouphes, and M. A. Smyer. 2005. "The Diverse Employment Experiences of Older Men and Women in the Workforce (Research Highlight No. 02)." Chestnut Hill, MA: Center on Aging & Work/Workplace Flexibility. Retrieved (http://agingandwork. bc.edu/documents/RH02_DiverseEmployExper.pdf).

Bureau of Census. 2011. "1948–2011 Current Population Survey". Retrieved October 26, 2012 (http://thedataweb.rm.census.gov/ftp/cps_ftp.html).

Bureau of Labor Statistics. 2009. "Nonfatal Occupational Injuries and Illnesses Requiring Days Away from Work, 2008." Washington, DC: Bureau of Labor Statistics. Retrieved October 26, 2012 (http://www.bls.gov/news.release/osh2.nr0.htm).

———. 2010a. "Characteristics of Minimum Wage Workers: 2009." Washington, DC: Bureau of Labor Statistics. Retrieved October 26, 2012 (http://www.bls.gov/cps/minwage2009.htm).

———. 2010b. "Number of Jobs Held, Labor Market Activity, and Earnings Growth among the Youngest Baby Boomers: Results from a Longitudinal Survey Summary." Washington, DC: Bureau of Labor Statistics. Retrieved October 26, 2012 (http://www.bls.gov/news.release/nlsoy. nr0.htm).

———. 2010c. "Persons with a Disability: Labor Force Characteristics Summary." Washington, DC: Bureau of Labor Statistics. Retrieved (http://www.bls.gov/news.release/disabl.nr0.htm).

———. 2010d. "Program Perspectives on Benefits by Wage Level (Vol. 2, Issue No. 1)." Washington, DC: Bureau of Labor Statistics. Retrieved October 26, 2012 (http://www.bls.gov/opub/perspectives/ program_perspectives_vol2_issue1.pdf).

———. 2010e. "Worker Displacement: 2007–2009." Washington, DC: Bureau of Labor Statistics. Retrieved October 26, 2012 (http://www.bls.gov/news.release/pdf/disp.pdf).

———. 2011. "Volunteering in the United States—2010." Washington, DC: Bureau of Labor Statistics. Retrieved October 26, 2012 (http://www.bls.gov/news.release/pdf/volun.pdf).

———. 2012a. "Current Population Survey." Retrieved (http://www.bls.gov/news.release/pdf/wkyeng.pdf).

———. 2012b. "Employee Benefits Survey." Retrieved October 26, 2012 (http://data.bls.gov/cgi-bin/dsrv?eb).

Burkhauser, R. V., and J. F. Quinn. 1997. *Pro-work Policy Proposals for Older Americans in the 21st Century (Policy Brief No. 9)*. Syracuse, NY: Syracuse University Maxwell School of Citizenship and Public Affairs.

Butrica, B. A., R. W. Johnson, and S. R. Zedlewski. 2009. "Volunteer Dynamics of Older Americans." *Journal of Gerontology: Social Sciences 64B*: 644–55. doi: 10.1093/geronb/gbn042.

Caban-Martinez, A. J., D. J. Lee, L. E. Fleming, D. J. Tancredi, K. L. Arheart, W. G. LeBlanc, and P. A. Muennig. 2011. Arthritis, Occupational Class, and the Aging U.S. Workforce. *American Journal of Public Health 10*: 1729–34. doi: 10.2105/AJPH.2011.300173.

Cahill, K. E., M. D. Giandrea, and J. F. Quinn. 2007. "Down Shifting: The Role of Bridge Jobs after Career Employment." *Issue Brief No. 6*. Chestnut Hill, MA: Boston College Center on Aging & Work/Workplace Flexibility. Retrieved (http://agingandwork.bc.edu/documents/IB06_DownShifting_003.pdf).

Callahan, J. S., D. S. Kiker, and T. Cross. 2003. "Does Method Matter? A Meta-analysis of the Effects of Training Method on Older Learner Training Performance." *Journal of Management 29*: 663–80. doi: 10.1016/S0149-2063_03_00029-1.

Careerbuilder. 2011. "Fewer Workers Age 60 and Up Postponing Retirement, Finds New Careerbuilder Survey." Retrieved January 29, 2011 (http://www.careerbuilder.com/share/aboutus/pressreleasesdetail.aspx?id=pr617&sd=1%2f26%2f2011&ed=1%2f26%2f2011&siteid=cbpr&sc_cmp1=cb_pr617_).

Carstensen, L. L., D. M. Isaacowitz, and S. T. Charles. 1999. "Taking Time Seriously: A Theory of Socioemotional Selectivity." *American Psychologist 54*: 165–81.

Celis, J. 2010. "Disparities in Automatic Enrollment Plan Availability." Washington, DC: Bureau of Labor Statistics. Retrieved October 26, 2012 (http://www.bls.gov/opub/cwc).

Centers for Disease Control and Prevention. 1999. "Vital Statistics of the United States Detailed Table 1-1: Live Births, Birth Rates, and Fertility Rates, by Race, 1909–94." Washington, DC: Centers for Disease Control and Prevention. Retrieved October 26, 2012 (http://www.cdc.gov/nchs/data/statab/t941x01.pdf).

———. 2009. "Prevalence and Most Common Causes of Disability Among Adults—United States, 2005." *Morbidity and Mortality Weekly Report 58*: 421–26. Washington, DC: Centers for Disease Control and Prevention. Retrieved October 26, 2012 (http://www.cdc.gov/mmwr/preview/mmwrhtml/mm5816a2.htm).

Chiteji, N. S., and F. P. Stafford. 1999. "Portfolio Choices of Parents and Their Children as Young Adults: Asset Accumulation by African-American Families." *American Economic Review 89(2)*: 377–80.

Choi, J. N. 2007. "Group Composition and Employee Creative Behavior in a Korean Electronics Company: Distinct Effects of Relational Demography and Group Diversity." *Journal of Occupational and Organizational Psychology 80*: 213–34. doi: 10.1348/096317906X110250.

Choi, N. G., J. A. Burr, J. E. Mutchler, and F. G. Caro. 2007. "Formal and Informal Volunteer Activity and Spousal Caregiving among Older Adults." *Research on Aging 29*: 99–124. doi: 10.1177/0164027506296759.

Choudhury, S. 2001/2002. "Racial and Ethnic Differences in Wealth and Asset Choices." *Social Security Bulletin 64*(4): 1–15. (http://www.socialsecurity.gov/policy/docs/ssb/v64n4/v64n4p1.pdf).

Civil Rights Act of 1964 § 7, 42 U.S.C. § 2000e et seq. 1964.

Collins, M. H., J. F. Hair, and T. S. Rocco. 2009. "The Older-worker–Younger-supervisor Dyad: A Test of the Reverse Pygmalion Effect." *Human Resource Development Quarterly 20*: 21–41. doi: 10.1002/hrdq.20006.

Copeland, C. 2011. "Labor-force Participation Rates of the Population Age 55 and Older: What Did the Recession Do to the Trends?" *EBRI Notes 32(2)*: 8–16. Retrieved October 26, 2012 (http://www.ebri.org/pdf/notespdf/EBRI_Notes_02_Feb-11.HCS_Part-Rts.pdf).

Corak, M. 2006. "Do Poor Children Become Poor Adults?" Pp. 143–88 in *Dynamics of Inequality and Poverty*, ed. J. Creedy and G. Kalb. Boston, MA: Elsevier.

Cornwell, B. 2011. "Age Trends in Daily Social Contact Patterns." *Research on Aging 33*: 598–631. doi: 10.1177/0164027511409442.

Costa, D. 1998. *The Evolution of Retirement: An American Economic History 1880–1990*. Chicago, IL: University of Chicago Press.

Crowley, J. E. 1986. "Longitudinal Effects of Retirement on Men's Well-being and Health." *Journal of Business and Psychology 2*: 95–113. doi: 10.1007/BF01018806.

Dalirazar, N. 2007. "Reasons People Do Not Work: 2004 (Current Population Reports No. P70-111)." Washington, DC: U.S. Census Bureau. Retrieved October 26, 2012 (http://www.census.gov/prod/2007pubs/p70-111.pdf).

DeLong, D. 2006. "Living Longer, Working Longer: The Changing Landscape of the Aging Workforce—A MetLife Study." New York, NY: MetLife Mature Market Institute. Retrieved October 26, 2012 (http://www.metlife.com/assets/cao/mmi/publications/studies/mmi-studies-living-longer.pdf).

Eaton, S. C. 2003. "If You Can Use Them: Flexibility Policies, Organizational Commitment, and Perceived Performance." *Industrial Relations 42*: 145–67. doi: 10.1111/1468-232X.00285.

Edwards, K., and H. Shierholz. 2010. "Leaving in Droves." *Economic Snapshot No. 02-24*. Washington, DC: Economic Policy Institute. Retrieved October 26, 2012 (http://www.epi.org/economic_snapshots/entry/leaving_in_droves.)

Engelhardt, G. V., and A. Kumar. 2007. "The Repeal of the Retirement Earnings Test and the Labor Supply of Older Men." *Working Paper 2007-1*. Chestnut Hill, MA: Center for Retirement Research.

Even, W., and D. MacPherson. 2007. "Defined Contribution Pension Plans and the Distribution of Pension Wealth." *Industrial Relations 46*: 551–81. doi: 10.1111/j.1468-232X.2007.00480.x.

Eyster, L., R. W. Johnson, and E. Toder. 2008. "Current Strategies to Employ and Retain Older Workers." Washington, DC: The Urban Institute. Retrieved October 26, 2012 (http://www.urban.org/UploadedPDF/411626_olderworkers.pdf).

Federal Interagency Forum on Aging-Related Statistics. 2010. *Older Americans 2010*: Key Indicators of Well-being. Washington, DC: U.S. Government Printing Office. Retrieved October 26, 2012 (http://www.agingstats.gov/agingstatsdotnet/Main_Site/Data/2010_Documents/Docs/OA_2010.pdf).

Ferraro, K. F., and T. P. Shippee. 2009. "Aging and Cumulative Inequality: How Does Inequality Get Under the Skin?" *The Gerontologist 49*: 333–43. doi: 10.1093/geront/gnp034.

Frazis, H., M. Gittleman and M. Joyce. 1998. "Correlates of Training: An Analysis Using Both Employer and Employee Characteristics." *Industrial and Labor Relations Review 53*: 443–62.

Friedberg, L. 2000. "The Labor Supply Effects of the Social Security Earnings Test." *Review of Economics and Statistics 82*: 48–63.

Friedberg, L., and A. Webb. 2005. "Retirement and the Evolution of Pension Structure." *The Journal of Human Resources 40*: 281–308.

Fronstin, P. 2007. "Employment-based Health Benefits: Access and Coverage, 1988–2005." *Issue Brief No. 303*. Washington, DC: Employee Benefit Research Institute. Retrieved October 26, 2012 (http://www.ebri.org/pdf/briefspdf/EBRI_IB_03-20071.pdf).

Galinsky, E., J. T. Bond, and E. J. Hill. 2004. *When Work Works: A Ranking Report on Workplace Flexibility*. New York: Families and Work Institute.

Galunic, D., and E. Anderson. 2000. "From Security to Mobility: Generalized Investments in Human Capital and Agent Commitment." *Organizational Science 11*: 1–20.

Gattis, M., N. Morrow-Howell, S. McCrary, M. Lee, M. Jonson-Reid, H. McCoy, K. Tamar, A. Molina, and M. Invernizzi. 2010. "Examining the Effects of New York Experience Corps® Program on Young Readers." *Literary Research and Instruction 49*: 299–314. doi: 10.1080/19388070903117948.

Giandrea, M. D., K. E. Cahill, and J. F. Quinn. 2007. "An Update on Bridge Jobs: The HRS War Babies." *Working Paper No. 407*. Washington, DC: Bureau of Labor Statistics. Retrieved (http://www.bls.gov/osmr/pdf/ec070060.pdf).

Gibson, R. C. 1987. "Reconceptualizing Retirement for Black Americans." *The Gerontologist 27(6)*: 691–98.

Goldberg, C. B. 2005. "Relational Demography and Similarity-attraction in Interview Assessments and Subsequent Offer Decisions: Are We Missing Something?" *Group and Organization Management 30*: 597–624. doi: 10.1177/1059601104267661.

Golden, L. 2009. "Flexible Daily Work Schedules in U.S. Jobs: Formal Introductions Needed?" *Industrial Relations 48*: 27–54. doi: 10.1111/j.1468-232X.2008.00544.x.

Gonyea, J. G. 2007. "Improving the Retirement Prospects of Lower-wage Workers in a Defined-contribution World." *Families in Society: The Journal of Contemporary Social Services 88*: 453–62. doi: 10.1606/1044-3894.3655.

Gould, E. 2011. "Access to Sick Days is Vastly Unequal." Washington, DC: Economic Policy Institute. Retrieved October 26, 2012 (http://www.epi.org/economic_snapshots/entry/access_to_sick_days_is_vastly_unequal).

Gratton, L., A. Voight, and T. J. Erickson. 2007. "Bridging Faultlines in Diverse Teams." *MIT Sloan Management Review 48(4)*: 22–29. doi: 10.1109/EMR.2011.5729976.

Greenfield, E. M., and N. F. Marks. 2010. "Identifying Experiences of Physical and Psychological Violence in Childhood that Jeopardize Mental Health in Adulthood." *Child Abuse & Neglect 34*: 161–71. doi: 10.1016/j.chiabu.2009.08.012.

Greenwood, J., and A. Seshadri. 2002. "The U.S. Demographic Transition." *American Economic Review* 92: 153–59. doi: 10.1257/000282802320189168.

Groeneman, S. 2008. "Staying Ahead of the Curve 2007: The AARP Work and Career Study." Washington, DC: AARP. Retrieved October 26, 2012 (http://assets.aarp.org/rgcenter/econ/work_career_08.pdf).

Guralnik, J. M., S. Butterworth, M. E. J. Wadsworth, and D. Kuh. 2006. "Childhood Socioeconomic Status Predicts Physical Functioning a Half Century Later." *Journals of Gerontology: Series A: Biological Sciences and Medical Sciences* 61: 694–701. doi: 10.1093/Gerona/61.7.694.

Gustman, A. L., and T. Steinmeier. 2009. "How Changes in Social Security Affect Recent Retirement Trends." *Research on Aging* 31: 261–90. doi: 10.1177/0164027508328312.

Haas, S. 2008. "Trajectories of Functional Health: The 'Long Arm' of Childhood Health and Socio-economic Factors." *Social Science & Medicine* 66: 849–61. doi: 10.1016/j.socscimed.2007.11.004.

Haas, S., and L. Rohlfsen. 2010. "Life Course Determinants of Racial and Ethnic Disparities in Functional Health Trajectories." *Social Science and Medicine* 70: 240–50. doi: 10.1016/j.socscimed.2009.10.003.

Heidkamp, M., N. Corre, and C. E. Van Horn. 2010. "The 'New Unemployables': Older Job Seekers Struggle to Find Work During the Great Recession." *Issue Brief No. 25*. Chestnut Hill, MA: The Sloan Center on Aging & Work. Retrieved October 26, 2012 (http://www.bc.edu/content/dam/files/research_sites/agingandwork/pdf/publications/IB25_NewUnemployed.pdf).

Heidkamp, M., and C. E. Van Horn. 2008. "Older and Out of Work: Employer, Government and Nonprofit Assistance." *Issue Brief No. 17*. Chestnut Hill, MA: Sloan Center on Aging & Work at Boston College. Retrieved October 26, 2012 (http://agingandwork.bc.edu/documents/IB17_Older&OutofWork2.pdf).

Helman, R., C. Copeland, and J. VanDerhei. 2009. "The 2009 Retirement Confidence Survey: Economy Drives Confidence to Record Lows; Many Looking to Work Longer." *Issue Brief No. 328*. Washington, DC: Employee Benefit Research Institute. Retrieved October 26, 2012 (http://www.ebri.org/pdf/briefspdf/EBRI_IB_4-2009_RCS1.pdf).

Helman, R., C. Copeland, and J. VanDerhei. 2011. "The 2011 Retirement Confidence Survey: Confidence Drops to Record Lows, Reflecting 'The New Normal.' *Issue Brief No. 355*. Washington, DC: Employee Benefit Research Institute. Retrieved October 26, 2012 (http://www.ebri.org/pdf/briefspdf/EBRI_03-2011_No355_RCS-2011.pdf).

Helman, R., C. Copeland, J. VanDerhei, and D. Salisbury. 2008. "EBRI 2008 Recent Retirees Survey: Report of Findings." *Issue Brief No. 319*. Washington, DC: Employee Benefit Research Institute. Retrieved October 26, 2012 (http://www.ebri.org/pdf/briefspdf/EBRI_IB_07-2008.pdf).

Hendrie H. C., M. S. Albert, M. A. Butters, S. Gao, D. S. Knopman, L. J. Launer, K. Yaffe, B. N. Cuthbert, E. Edwards, and M. V. Wagster. 2006. "The NIH Cognitive and Emotional Health Project: Report of the Critical Evaluation Study Committee." *Alzheimers & Dementia 2*: 12–32.

Hewitt Associates. 2008. "Retiring Boomers Prompt Increased Employer Interest in Phased Retirement Programs, According to Hewitt Survey." Lincolnshire, IL: Hewitt Associates. Retrieved October 26, 2012 (http://www.hewittassociates.com/Intl/NA/en-US/AboutHewitt/Newsroom/PressReleaseDetail.aspx?cid=5451).

Hewlett, S. A., M. Jackson, L. Sherbin, P. Shiller, E. Sosnovich, and K. Sumberg. 2009. *Bookend Generations: Leveraging Talent and Finding Common Ground.* New York: Center for Work-Life Policy.

Holmes, J., E. Powell-Griner, M. Lethbridge-Cejku, and K. Heyman. 2009. "Aging Differently: Physical Limitations among Adults Ages 50 Years and Over: United States, 2001–2007." *NCHS Data Brief No. 20.* Hyattsville, MD: National Center for Health Statistics. Retrieved October 26, 2012 (http://www.globalaging.org/health/us/2009/physicallimitations.pdf).

Hutchens, R. 2003. "The Cornell Study of Employer Phased Retirement Policies: A Report on Key Findings." Ithaca, NY: Cornell University, School of Industrial and Labor Relations. Retrieved October 26, 2012 (http://digitalcommons.ilr.cornell.edu/cgi/viewcontent.cgi?article=1000&context=lepubs).

Hutchens, R., and J. Chen. 2006. "Phased Retirement: Opportunities for Some, But Not for All." *ILR Impact Brief No. 3.* Ithaca, NY: School of Industrial and Labor Relations, Cornell University.

Issa, P., and S. R. Zedlewski. 2011. "Poverty among Older Americans, 2009." *Retirement Data Security Brief No. 2011-1.* Washington, DC: Urban Institute. Retrieved October 26, 2012 (http://www.urban.org/uploadedpdf/412296-Poverty-Among-Older-Americans.pdf).

Johnson, R. W., M. Favreault, and C. Mommaerts. 2009. "Work Ability and the Social Insurance Safety Net in the Years Prior to Retirement." *Working Paper No. WP 2009-28.* Chestnut Hill, MA: Center for Retirement Research at Boston College. Retrieved October 26, 2012 (http://crr.bc.edu/wp-content/uploads/2009/11/wp_2009-28-508.pdf).

Johnson, R. W., and J. Kawachi. 2007. *Job Changes at Older Ages: Effects on Wages, Benefits, and Other Job Attributes.* Washington, DC: Urban Institute. Retrieved October 26, 2012 (http://www.urban.org/UploadedPDF/311435_Job_Changes.pdf).

Johnson, R. W., J. Kawachi, and E. K. Lewis. 2009. "Older Workers on the Move: Recareering in Later Life." *Research Report No. 2009-08.* Washington, DC: AARP Public Policy Institute. Retrieved October 26, 2012 (http://assets.aarp.org/rgcenter/econ/2009_08_recareering.pdf).

Johnson, R. W., and C. Mommaerts. 2011. "Age Differences in Job Loss, Job Search, and Reemployment." *Program on Retirement Policy Discussion Paper No. 11-01.* Washington, DC: Urban Institute. Retrieved October 26, 2012 (http://crr.bc.edu/wp-content/uploads/2011/01/wp_2011-3.pdf).

Johnson, R. W., and M. Soto. 2009. "50+ Hispanic Workers: A Growing Segment of the U.S. Workforce." Washington, DC: AARP. Retrieved October 26, 2012 (http://assets.aarp.org/rgcenter/econ/hispanic_workers_09.pdf).

Kahn, J. R., B. S. McGill, and S. M. Bianchi. 2011. "Help to Family and Friends: Are There Gender Differences at Older Ages?" *Journal of Marriage and Family 73*: 77–92. doi: 10.1111/j.1741-3737.2010.00790.x.

Koppen, J. 2010. "Social Media and Technology Use among Adults 50+." Washington, DC: AARP. Retrieved October 26, 2012 (http://assets.aarp.org/rgcenter/general/socmedia.pdf).

Koppen, J., and G. Anderson. 2008. "Retired Spouses: A National Survey of Adults 55–75." Washington, DC: AARP. Retrieved October 26, 2012 (http://assets.aarp.org/rgcenter/general/retired_spouses.pdf).

Lahey, J. 2005. "Age, Women, and Hiring: An Experimental Study." *Working Paper No. 11435*. Washington, DC: National Bureau of Economic Research. Retrieved October 26, 2012 (http://www.nber.org/papers/w11435).

Lashbrook, J. 1995. "Promotional Timetables: An Exploratory Investigation of Age Norms for Promotional Expectations and their Association with Job Well-being." *The Gerontologist 36*: 189–98. doi: 10.1093/geront/36.2.189.

Lawrence, B. S. 1995. "Organizational Age Norms: Why Is It So Hard to Know One When You See One?" *The Gerontologist 36*: 209–20. doi: 10.1093/geront/36.2.209.

Lee, S., and L. Shaw. 2008. "From Work to Retirement: Tracking Changes in Women's Poverty." Washington, DC: AARP. Retrieved October 26, 2012 (http://assets.aarp.org/rgcenter/econ/2008_03_poverty.pdf).

Lee, Y. S., N. Morrow-Howell, M. Johnson-Reid, and S. McCrary. 2010. "The Effect of the Experience Corps Program on Student Reading Outcomes." *Education and Urban Society 20*: 1–22. doi: 10.1177/0013124510381262.

Livingston, G., and K. Parker. 2010. "Since the Start of the Great Recession, More Children Raised by Grandparents." Washington, DC: Pew Research Center. Retrieved October 26, 2012 (http://pewsocialtrends.org/assets/pdf/764-children-raised-by-grandparents.pdf).

Lyketsos, C. G. 2006. "Commentary on 'The NIH Cognitive and Emotional Health Project: Report of the Critical Evaluation Study Committee. What Would be the Effect of Raising the Retirement Age by Five Years on the Cognitive and Emotional Health of Individuals Age 65 and Older?" *Alzheimers & Dementia 2*: 86–88. doi: 10.1016/j.jalz.2006.01.001.

Maestas, Nicole. 2007. "Back to Work: Expectations and Realizations of Work after Retirement." *Working Paper No. WR-196-2*. Arlington, VA: Rand Corporation. Retrieved October 26, 2012 (http://www.rand.org/pubs/working_papers/2007/RAND_WR196-2.pdf).

Mastrobuoni, G. 2006. "The Social Security Earnings Test Removal: Money Saved or Money Spent by the Trust Fund?" *CEPS Working Paper No. 133*. Princeton, NJ: Princeton University Center for Economic Policy Studies. Retrieved October 26, 2012 (http://www.princeton.edu/~ceps/workingpapers/133mastrobuoni.pdf).

MetLife. 2009a. "Buddy, Can You Spare a Job? The New Realities of the Job Market for Aging Baby Boomers." Westport, CT: MetLife. Retrieved October 26, 2012 (http://www.metlife.com/assets/cao/mmi/publications/studies/mmi-buddy-can-you-spare-job.pdf).

———. 2009b. "MetLife Emerging Retirement Model Study: A Survey of Plan Sponsors." New York: MetLife. Retrieved October 26, 2012 (https://www.metlife.com/assets/institutional/services/cbf/retirement/EmergRetireModelStudy_0912.pdf).

———. 2009c. "Study of Employee Benefits Trends: Findings from the 7th Annual National Survey of Employers and Employees." New York, NY: MetLife. Retrieved October 26, 2012 (http://whymetlife.com/trends/downloads/MetLife_EBTS09.pdf).

———. 2011. "The MetLife Study of Caregiving Costs to Working Caregivers: Double Jeopardy for Baby Boomers Caring for their Parents." Westport, CT: MetLife. Retrieved October 26, 2012 (http://www.metlife.com/assets/cao/mmi/publications/studies/2011/mmi-caregiving-costs-working-caregivers.pdf).

Miller, S. J. 1965. "The Social Dilemma of the Aging Leisure Participant." Pp. 77–92 in *Older People and Their Social World*, ed. A. Rose. Philadelphia, PA: F. A. Davis.

Morin, R., and R. Kochbar. 2010. "The Impact of Long-term Unemployment: Lost Income, Lost Friends—and Loss of Self-respect." Washington, DC: Pew Research Center. Retrieved October 26, 2012 (http://pewsocialtrends.org/assets/pdf/760-recession.pdf).

Muller, L. A., J. H. Moore Jr, and K. R. Elliott. 2009. "Who is Likely to Opt Out of an Automatic Enrollment Plan? Who is Likely to Stay In?: A Study of 401(k) Participation Choices." *Benefits Quarterly 25*: 47–62.

Munnel, A. H., A. Webb, and F. Golub-Sass. 2007. "Is There Really a Retirement Savings Crisis? An NRRI Analysis." *Issue Brief No. 7-11*. Chestnut Hill, MA: Center for Retirement Research at Boston College. Retrieved October 26, 2012 (http://crr.bc.edu/wp-content/uploads/2007/07/ib_7-11.pdf).

Munnell, A. H., S. Sass, and M. Soto. 2006. "Employer Attitudes towards Older Workers: Survey Results." *Issue Brief No. WOB-3*. Chestnut Hill, MA: Center for Retirement Research at Boston College. Retrieved October 26, 2012 (http://crr.bc.edu/wp-content/uploads/2006/07/wob_3.pdf).

Munnell, A. H., and A. Sundén. 2006. "401(k) Plans are Still Coming Up Short." *Issue Brief 43*. Chestnut Hill, MA: Center for Retirement Research at Boston College. Retrieved October 26, 2012 (http://crr.bc.edu/wp-content/uploads/2006/03/ib_43.pdf).

Mutchler, J. E., J. A. Burr, and F. G. Caro. 2003. "From Paid Worker to Volunteer: Leaving the Paid Workforce and Volunteering in Later Life." *Social Forces 8*: 1267–93. doi: 10.1353/sof.2003.0067.

National Alliance for Caregiving, AARP, and MetLife. 2009. "Caregiving in the U.S.: A Focused Look at those Caring for the 50+." Bethesda, MD: National Alliance for Caregiving. Retrieved October 26, 2012 (http://www.caregiving.org/data/2009CaregivingAARP_Full_Report.pdf).

National Institute of Health. 1996. "Physical Activity and Cardiovascular Health: NIH Consensus Development Panel on Physical Activity and Cardiovascular Health." *Journal of the American Medical Association 276(3)*: 241–6.

Neuman, K. 2008. "Quit Your Job and Get Healthier? The Effect of Retirement on Health." *Journal of Labor Research 29*: 117–201. doi: 10.1007/s12122-007-9036-8.

Neumark, D. 2009. "The Age Discrimination in Employment Act and the Challenge of Population Aging." *Research on Aging 31*: 41–68. doi: 10.1177/0164027508324640.

Neumark, D., and W. A. Stock. 1999. "Age Discrimination Laws and Labor Market Efficiency." *Journal of Political Economy 107*: 1081–25. doi: 10.1086/250091.

Nishii, L. H., and D. M. Mayer. 2009. "Do Inclusive Leaders Help to Reduce Turnover in Diverse Groups? The Moderating Role of Leader–Member Exchange in the Diversity to Turnover Relationship." *Journal of Applied Psychology 94*: 1412–26. doi: 10.1037/a0017190.

O'Berg, C. 2003. "The Impact of Childhood Poverty on Health and Development." *Healthy Generations 4(1)*: 1–3. Retrieved October 26, 2012 (http://www.epi.umn.edu/mch/resources/hg/hg_childpoverty.pdf).

Parkinson, D. 2002. *Voices of Experience: Mature Workers in the Future Workforce*. New York, NY: The Conference Board.

Pelled, L. H., K. M. Eisenhardt, and K. R. Xin. 1999. "Exploring The Black Box: An Analysis of Work Group Diversity, Conflict, and Performance." *Administrative Science Quarterly 44*: 1–28. doi: 10.2307/2667029.

Perron, R. 2010. "Recession Takes Toll on Hispanics 45+: Boomers Particularly Hard Hit." Washington, DC: AARP. Retrieved October 26, 2012 (http://assets.aarp.org/rgcenter/econ/hispeconomy. pdf).

Pew Research Center. 2010. "Millennials: A Portrait of Generation Next." Washington, DC: The Pew Research Center. Retrieved October 26, 2012 (http://pewsocialtrends.org/assets/pdf/millennials-confident-connected-open-to-change.pdf).

Powell, Walter W., and Paul J. DiMaggio, eds. 1991. *The New Institutionalism in Organizational Analysis*. Chicago, IL: University Press.

Purcell, P. 2009. "Income and Poverty among Older Americans in 2008." Washington, DC: Congressional Research Service. Retrieved October 26, 2012 (http://assets.opencrs.com/rpts/ RL32697_20091002.pdf).

Quadagno, J. 1982. *Aging in Early Industrial Society: Work, Family, and Social Policy in Nineteenth-century England*. New York: Academic Press.

Ranstad Work Solutions. 2007. "The World of Work 2007." Rochester, NY: Harris Interactive, Inc. Retrieved October 26, 2012 (http://us.randstad.com/content/aboutrandstad/knowledge-center/ employer-resources/World-of-Work-2007.pdf).

Ratcliffe, C., and S. McKernan. 2010. "Childhood Poverty Persistence: Facts and Consequences." *Brief No. 14*. Washington, DC: The Urban Institute. Retrieved October 26, 2012 (http://www.urban. org/UploadedPDF/412126-child-poverty-persistence.pdf).

Reitzes, D. C., and E. J. Mutran. 2006. "Lingering Identities in Retirement." *The Sociological Quarterly* 47: 333–59. doi: 10.1111/j.1533-8525.2006.00048.x.

Reitzes, D. C., E. J. Mutran, and M. E. Fernandez. 1996. "Does Retirement Hurt Well-being? Factors Influencing Self-esteem and Depression among Retirees and Workers." *The Gerontologist 36*: 649–56.

Restrepo, T., S. Sobel, and H. Shuford. 2006. "Age as a Driver of Frequency and Severity." *NCCI Research Brief*. Boca Raton, FL: National Council on Compensation Insurance. Retrieved (http:// www.ncci.com/Documents/research_age_frequency.pdf).

Reynolds, S., N. Ridley, and C. Van Horn. 2005. "A Work-filled Retirement: Workers' Changing Views on Employment and Leisure." *Work Trends Survey No. 8.1*. New Brunswick, NJ: John J. Heldrich Center for Workforce Development, Rutgers University. Retrieved October 26, 2012 (http:// www.heldrich.rutgers.edu/sites/default/files/content/WT16.pdf).

Rho, H. J. 2010. "Hard Work? Patterns in Physically Demanding Labor among Older Workers." Washington, DC: Center for Economic and Policy Research. Retrieved (http://www.cepr.net/ documents/publications/older-workers-2010-08.pdf).

Rijs, K. J., Cozijnsen, R., and Deeg, D. J. H. 2012. "The Effect of Retirement and Age at Retirement on Self-perceived Health after Three Years of Follow-up in Dutch 55–64 Year-olds." *Ageing & Society 32*: 281–306.

Rix, S. E. 1996. "Investing in the Future: What Role for Older Worker Training?" Pp. 304–23 in *Handbook on Employment and the Elderly*, ed. W. H. Crown. Westport, CT: Greenwood Press.

Rix, S. E. 2011. "The Employment Situation, September 2011: Good News for Older Jobseekers Remains Elusive." *Fact Sheet No. 240*. Washington, DC: AARP Public Policy Institute. Retrieved October 26, 2012 (http://assets.aarp.org/rgcenter/ppi/econ-sec/fs240-economic.pdf).

Rousseau, D. 1995. *Psychological Contracts in Organisations: Understanding Written and Unwritten Agreements.* Thousand Oaks, CA: Sage.

Shaw, B. A., N. Krause, J. Liang, and J. Bennett. 2007. "Tracking Changes in Social Relations throughout Late Life." *Journal of Gerontology Series B: Psychological Sciences and Social Sciences 62B*: S90-9. doi: 10.1093/geronb/62.2.S90.

Shrestha, L. B. 2006. *Specialist in Demography CRS Report for Congress: Life Expectancy in the United States.* Retrieved October 26, 2012 (http://aging.senate.gov/crs/aging1.pdf).

Shuey, K. M., and A. E. Willson. 2008. "Cumulative Disadvantage and Black–White Disparities in Life-course Health Trajectories." *Research on Aging 30*: 200–25. doi: 10.1177/0164027507311151.

Simpson, P. A., M. M. Greller, and L. K. Stroh. 2002. "Variations in Human Capital Investment Activity by Age." *Journal of Vocational Behavior 61*: 109–38. doi: 10.1006/jvbe.2001.1847.

Slack, T., and Jensen, L. (2008). "Employment Hardship among Older Workers: Does Residential and Gender Inequality Extend into Older Age?" *Journals of Gerontology 63*: S15–S24. doi: 10.1093/geronb/63.1.S15.

Social Security Administration. 2011. "Fast Facts & Figures about Social Security, 2011." *SSA Publication No. 13-11785.* Washington, DC: Social Security Administration. Retrieved October 26, 2012 (http://www.ssa.gov/policy/docs/chartbooks/fast_facts/2011/fast_facts11.pdf).

Society for Human Resource Management. 2010. "2010 Employee Benefits: Examining Employee Benefits in the Midst of a Recovering Economy." Alexandria, VA: Society for Human Resource Management. Retrieved October 26, 2012 (http://www.shrm.org/research/surveyfindings/articles/documents/10-0280%20employee%20benefits%20survey%20report-fnl.pdf).

Sparrow, P. R., and D. R. Davies. 1988. "Effects of Age, Tenure, Training, and Job Complexity on Technical Performance." *Psychology and Aging 3*: 307–14.

Stewart, M. M., and P. Garcia-Prieto. 2008. "A Relational Demography Model of Workgroup Identification: Testing the Effects of Race, Race Dissimilarity, Racial Identification, and Communication Behavior." *Journal of Organizational Behavior 29*: 657–80. doi: 10.1002/job.523.

Swaen, G. M. H., I. Kant, L. G. P. M. van Amelsvoort, and A. J. H. M. Beurskens. 2002. "Job Mobility, Its Determinants, and Its Effects: Longitudinal Data from the Maastricht Cohort Study." *Journal of Occupational Health Psychology 7*: 121–29.

Swanberg, J. E., M. Pitt-Catsouphes, and K. Drescher-Burke. 2005. "A Question of Justice: Disparities in Employees' Access to Flexible Schedule Arrangements." *Journal of Family Issues 26*: 866–95.

Tansky, J. W., and D. J. Cohen. 2001. "The Relationship between Organizational Support, Employee Development, and Organizational Commitment: An Empirical Study." *Human Resource Development Quarterly 12*: 285–300.

Taylor, P., and R. Morin. 2009. "Forty Years after Woodstock, A Gentler Generation Gap." Washington, DC: Pew Research Center. Retrieved October 26, 2012 (http://pewsocialtrends.org/assets/pdf/after-woodstock-gentler-generation-gap.pdf).

Taylor, P., R. Morin, K. Parker, and W. Wang. 2009. "Growing Old in America: Expectations vs. Reality." Washington, DC: Pew Research Center. Retrieved October 26, 2012 (http://www.pewsocialtrends.org/2009/06/29/growing-old-in-america-expectations-vs-reality).

Thayer, C. 2008. "Retirement Security or Insecurity? The Experience of Workers Aged 45 and Older." Washington, DC: AARP Knowledge Management. Retrieved (http://assets.aarp.org/rgcenter/econ/retirement_survey_08.pdf).

Thompson, C. A., L. L. Beauvais, and K. S. Lyness. 1999. "When Work–Family Benefits are Not Enough: The Influence of Work–Family Culture on Benefit Utilization, Organizational Attachment, and Work–Family Conflict." *Journal of Vocational Behavior 54*: 392–415. doi: 10.1006/jvbe.1998.1681.

Toosi, M. 2009. "Labor Force Projections to 2018: Older Workers Staying More Active." *Monthly Labor Review 132(11)*: 30–51.

Towers Perrin. 2005. "The Business Case for Workers Age 50+: Planning for Tomorrow's Talent Needs in Today's Competitive Environment." Washington, DC: AARP. Retrieved October 26, 2012 (http://assets.aarp.org/rgcenter/econ/workers_fifty_plus.pdf).

U.S. Census Bureau. 2005. *U.S. Census Bureau, Statistical Abstract of the United States: 2004–2005.* Washington, DC: U.S. Census Bureau.

———. 2012a. *State and County QuickFacts (Data derived from Population Estimates, American Community Survey, Census of Population and Housing, State and County Housing Unit Estimates, County Business Patterns, Nonemployer Statistics, Economic Census, Survey of Business Owners, Building Permits, Consolidated Federal Funds Report).* Washington, DC: U.S. Census Bureau. Retrieved October 26, 2012 (http://quickfacts.census.gov/qfd/states/00000.html).

———. 2012b. *The 2012 Statistical Abstract/The National Data Book.* Washington, DC: U.S. Census Bureau. Retrieved (http://www.census.gov/compendia/statab/cats/births_deaths_marriages_divorces/life_expectancy.html).

U.S. Equal Employment Opportunity Commission. 2010. "Charge Statistics FY 1997 through FY 2009." Washington, DC: U.S. Census Bureau. Retrieved (http://www.eeoc.gov/eeoc/statistics/enforcement/charges.cfm).

United States Government Accountability Office (GAO). 2011. *Income Security: Older Adults and the 2007–2009 Recession.* Washington, DC: U.S. Government Accountability Office. Retrieved October 26, 2012 (http://www.gao.gov/new.items/d1276.pdf).

Verba, S., K. L. Schlozman, and H. E. Brady. 1995. *Voice and Equality: Civic Volunteerism in American Politics.* Cambridge, MA: Harvard University Press.

Vincent, G. K., and V. Velkoff. 2010. "The Next Four Decades: The Older Population in the United States: 2010 to 2050." *Current Population Reports No. P25-1138.* Washington, DC: U.S. Census Bureau. Retrieved October 26, 2012 (http://www.census.gov/prod/2010pubs/p25-1138.pdf).

Wilson, J. (2000). Volunteering. *Annual Review of Sociology 26*: 215–40.

Wilson, J., and M. Musick. 1997. "Who Cares? Toward an Integrated Theory of Volunteer Work." *American Sociological Review 62*: 694–713.

World Health Organization. 2004. "The World Health Report 2004." Retrieved October 26, 2012 (http://www.who.int/whr/2004/en/report04_en.pdf).

WorldatWork. 2011. "Survey on Workplace Flexibility." Washington, DC: WorldatWork.Org. Retrieved October 26, 2012 (http://www.worldatwork.org/waw/adimLink?id=48161).

Xu, J., K. D. Kochanek, S. L. Murphy, and B. Tejada-Vera. 2010. "Deaths: Final Data for 2007." *National Vital Statistics Report 58(19).* Retrieved (http://www.cdc.gov/nchs/data/nvsr/nvsr58/nvsr58_19.pdf).

Yaffe, K., D. Barnes, M. Nevitt, L. Y. Lui, and K. Covinsky. 2001. "A Prospective Study of Physical Activity and Cognitive Decline in Elderly Women: Women Who Walk." *Archives of Internal Medicine 161*: 1703–08. doi: 10.1001/archinte.161.14.1703.

Yang, S., and M. Reid. 2006. "Adoption and Implementation of Flexible Work Program: A Cross-level Study." Paper presented at the Annual Meeting of the American Sociological Association, Montreal Convention Center, Montreal, Quebec, Canada Online. Retrieved (http://www.allacademic.com/meta/p94049_index.html).

Index

Page numbers followed by 't' refer to tables.

C

caregiving: unpaid help with basic needs and tasks; can refer to care provided to children, spouses, parents, other relatives, or nonrelatives 34, 35–36

Centers for Disease Control and Prevention 2, 12

childhood experiences influencing health 10, 12–13

class

see **socioeconomic status**

co-worker relationships 27, 28, 37

cumulative inequality: cumulative inequality is the idea that inequalities—both in advantages and in disadvantages—tend to accumulate from childhood to old age 10

and health 11–14

and wealth 14–17

D

debt 14

defined-benefit pensions: the pension is typically set at a level that takes into account final salary (or an average over the last few years) and the number of years working for the employer. The pension is funded by the employer, and employees typically cannot take the pension with them when they move between employers. If an employee leaves after only a few years he or she will often not be eligible for any pension benefits 6, 16

defined-contribution pensions: the final pension benefit is based on the cash balance in the employee's individual account at the time of retirement. Employees make contributions, often matched in part by contributions from the employer. The final value of the account will depend upon the amount contributed over the years and the returns based on how the assets were invested. The account can be transferred from one employer to another and is typically made up of a mixture of stocks and bonds. A 401K is a common type of defined-contribution pension 6, 16–17

disability: generally, refers to impairments in functioning. In relation to the workforce, disability often refers to impairments that interfere with an individual's ability to work 11, 12, 18

discrimination: differential or unfair treatment of an individual based on their real or perceived membership in a social category 3, 7, 29

see also **age discrimination**

displaced: workers are displaced if they have lost their jobs because their plant or company closed or moved, or because there was insufficient work 17, 20–21, 32

E

economic dependency ratio: the number of "dependents" (people not in the labor force) for every 100 "workers" (people in the labor force). It is typically defined in terms of age group, so that all individuals aged up to 14 as well as all individuals aged 65 or older are considered "dependents," and all other individuals are considered "workers," regardless of whether these people are actually working for pay 1

education: the level and type of formalized schooling that a person has completed xv
    and poverty 15–16, 16t

employer policies 5, 7, 24–25

employer-sponsored pensions: a general term referring to plans provided by employers to provide employees with income during retirement. There is a substantial amount of variation in the terms and generosity of such plans 3, 6, 7, 16–17
    see also **defined-benefit pensions**; **defined-contribution pensions**

ethnicity: typically refers to a group of people linked by a common heritage, language, or culture. It often overlaps with "race"
    see also **race**

F

family and community, effects of working longer on 35–38

financial resources: the amount of money available to an organization or individual, whether in the form of assets or income 9
    see also **assets**; **income**

flexible work options: employer-provided or sanctioned options that allow workers some latitude or control over the timing, amount, content, or location of their work 25

functional limitation: a health problem that is interfering with an individual's daily life, such as difficulty walking or climbing stairs 10, 12

G

gender: the psychological, social, cultural, and behavioral characteristics generally associated with each sex xv, 9, 28, 35
    education and income 15, 16t
    job losses and 21
    labor force participation rates and 3
    life expectancy and 2
    poverty and 14
    re-employment and 32
    retirement savings and 14
    underemployment and 24
    unemployment rates and 20t

generation: a group of individuals born over a specific time period, such as the baby boomers or Generation Y. People of the same generation tend to have experienced the same historical and cultural events, such as wars and technological advances, during their formative years. These events may have shaped their outlooks on and approaches to life. Because generations age together, it is often difficult to disentangle the effects of generation from the effects of age 8, 29, 30

government policies and programs 3, 5–6, 7

grandparents 32, 36

H

Health and Retirement Study 24

health: the physical and mental condition of a person 9
  and ability to work 10, 21–22
  and cumulative inequality 11–14
  link between wealth inequalities and 10–11
  working longer and 33–34
  see also **disability**; **functional limitation**; **morbidity**

health insurance: programs or policies intended to manage the risk of individual medical expenses 7, 13–14, 24, 26, 30
  see also **Medicare**

healthy life expectancies: the number of years that people can expect to live in full health 11

Hispanics 8–9, 12, 30
  health insurance 13, 14
  and job losses 21

human capital: the knowledge, skills, and abilities embodied in an individual 36

human resource strategies 7–8, 31–32

I

income: the amount of money that an individual or household receives over a given time frame, such as a year, from various sources, including wages, pensions, and annuities, and programs such as Social Security 7, 10, 14, 15, 17

institutional ageism: this form of ageism is embedded within organizational rules and practices 30

intermittent poverty: an individual, family, or household is in intermittent poverty if they fall below the poverty line occasionally 15

involuntary retirement: the result of factors such as poor health, lack of employment opportunities, or displacement from existing jobs, rather than from worker choice 19, 20–21, 22, 34

J

job security 31

jobs
  unequal access to 19–23
  unequal access to good 23–26

K

knowledge drain: the loss of accumulated knowledge where knowledge is held disproportionately by more established workers within an organization. Many businesses are concerned that as older workers retire in greater numbers, the business may experience excessive knowledge drain 7–8

L

labor force participation rate: the percentage of individuals either employed or looking for work, relative to the population as a whole. The labor force participation rate is often expressed for particular age groups, such as those aged 15 to 64 2, 3, 5, 25, 33
of adults aged 55 and over 4–5t
interrupted 17

life expectancy: the average number of years of life remaining at a particular age, such as at birth or at age 65 xiii, 2, 8–9
see also **healthy life expectancies**

M

mandatory retirement: requiring workers to leave their jobs at a certain number of years of tenure or at a certain age 5

Medicare: a nationally funded program ensuring access to health insurance to people aged 65 and older, as well as some other groups such as the disabled xiii, 3, 7

morbidity: a general term referring to disability or poor health 12

O

organizational timetables: the organizational beliefs about when a worker receives certain promotions or moves into certain types of jobs 28

P

persistent poverty: an individual, family, or household is in persistent poverty if they stay below the poverty line for several consecutive years or longer 15

phased retirement: the gradual reduction in number of hours worked or work responsibilities, leading up to full retirement 23, 25–26

population diversity 8–9

poverty: in general, poverty refers to a lack of economic or material resources. In the United States, poverty is defined in terms of income relative to household size. For instance, in 2012, a family of four would be considered in poverty if they had less than $23,000 a year in income 7, 12, 15–16
childhood 15
and education 15–16

by race and gender 14

see also **intermittent poverty**; **persistent poverty**

psychological contract: the implicit agreement about what constitutes a "fair" exchange between employees and employers 31

R

race: typically refers to a group of individuals linked by geographic ancestry or physical characteristics. It often overlaps with "ethnicity" 8–9

co-worker relationships and 28

education, employment and 15

health and 12, 13

and life expectancy 2, 8–9

and poverty 14

unemployment rate and 20

see also **ethnicity**

real wages: unlike nominal wages, these are wage amounts adjusted for inflation to allow accurate comparison over time 2, 19

recession of 2007-9 5, 14

retirement: generally refers to exit from the labor force among older adults. However, not all individuals define retirement in the same way. For instance, some workers might consider "exit from the labor force" to mean leaving a full-time job for a part-time job, while others might mean complete exit from all paid work 1

due to ill health 11

health in 33–34

reasons for postponing 33

self-esteem in 34–35

social connectedness in 35

trend towards earlier 1, 3, 5–6

well-being in 32–33

see also **involuntary retirement**; **mandatory retirement**; **phased retirement**

retirement savings 14–15, 16, 17

return on investment: a business metric measuring the improvement in profits relative to the amount of capital invested in a particular policy, program, or decision 31

reverse ageism: stereotypes directed against younger individuals 27, 29–30

reverse institutional ageism: reverse ageism embedded within organizational rules and practices 30

S

self-esteem 34–35

skills shortages 30

social capital: the social linkages through which an individual may gain knowledge or resources 18, 36

social connectedness 35

social norms: informal rules governing what is considered acceptable behavior within society 3

Social Security: in the context of this book, refers to the United States' federal Old- Age, Survivors, and Disability Insurance (OASDI) program, enacted as part of the Social Security Act of 1935. Primarily funded through payroll taxes, the majority of Social Security benefits are retirement benefits. Other countries have their own Social Security programs xiii, xiv, 3, 5–6, 7, 20

Social Security Reform Act 1983 xiv

socioeconomic status: an individual's or household's economic position, in terms of occupation, income, and education 12

stereotype: a belief about a person based on their membership in a social group 29

T

training 8, 31–32

U

underemployment: employment situations that are subpar relative to the standard, typically in number of hours worked 24

unemployment rate: the percentage of the population that is currently unemployed 20, 20t

unemployment: where people are without jobs, but are currently seeking employment 5, 17, 21, 34

and involuntary retirement 20–21

well being and 34

see also **displaced**

unintended consequences: the effects of social actions that are outside of their original purpose 27

and effects on family and community 35–38

and effects on well being 32–35

in workplace 27–32

V

volunteering: a form of unpaid work that is generally altruistic in nature. Certain organizations, including many nonprofits, are particularly reliant on volunteers 34, 36–38

W

wages 16t, 24, 30

see also **real wages**

wealth

link between health inequalities 10–11

and unequal chances to retire 14–17

well-being 32–35

working longer

and effects on family and community 35–38

and effects on well-being 32–35

and impact in workplace 27–32

importance of 6–8

as a result of economic recession 5

Y

younger workers 5, 7, 8, 23, 29, 30, 31–32